MW01268961

Weight Watchers Instant Pot Smart Points Cookbook

101 Delicious And Easy Weight Watchers Smart Points Recipes For Your Instant Pot To Fast Weight Loss And Improve Your Lifestyle

By Cliff Stone

Table of Contents

INTRODUCTION

Hi friend, this is Cliff Stone! Thank and congratulate you for purchasing this ultimate Weight Watchers Instant Pot Smart Points Cookbook. Hope you will find what you need!

If you are looking for a book about Weight Watchers program or Instant Pot cooking, if you are planning to lose weight rapidly and have a better life, if you are looking for some delicious recipes made in instant pot high pressure cooker and save you time & money! Then this book is right for you.

This book includes 3 parts. The part 1 is about Weight Watchers, which will tell you all the essential knowlegde of Weight Watcher program. You will be easily to follow this program by reading this part.

Part 2 is about Instant Pot! This part will be your guide of how to use instant pot effectively and properly. Many many useful advices you will find in this part! By following it, you will be professional of instant pot user!

Part 3 is 101 easy and delicious instant pot recipes for weight watchers program! All of these recipes have smart points, and most of them are in low score. You can easily find recipes that suit for you! Most of them are cooked in a short time and not in high price, which will save you much time and money!

With this complete guide of Weight Watchers Instant Pot Smart Points Cookbook, you will lose your weight permenantly! You will be slimmer, stronger and healthier! Wish you will have a pleasant journey of Weight Watchers Program!

PART 1: WHY WEIGHT WATCHERS?

WHAT IS WEIGHT WATCHER?

Weight Watchers is not a diet, but a system that guides you and educates you about healthy food and healthy choices in your life. Whilst Weight Watchers may not be your cup of tea, it is worth exploring and understanding, especially if you intend to use Weight Watchers recipes to lose weight. Millions of people have lost weight following the "Weight Watchers" program. Other diet fads have come and gone, but after 50 years, Weight Watchers is still going strong. Why? **Because the program is more than just a diet, it's a lifestyle, which leads to a healthy, happy, balanced individual.**

Weight Watchers is based on four essential pillars of weight loss namely **behaviour, food, support and exercise** and it is their constant attention to all four pillars which make the lifestyle successful. Their mantra is "the whole person matters" and they approach diet as a core part of the person.

This program is also adaptable to different people. It's no good telling a person who is four hundred pounds overweight to follow the same diet as someone who is close to their ideal weight. The diet would be unrealistic and the overweight person would never be able to follow the diet. They have therefore introduced various eating plans to suit just about every type of person. Weight Watchers also provides one thing which most other diet plans does not - **a huge level of motivation and support**. This is one of the reasons why the program is so successful. Dieting can often be demoralizing and a lonely experience, but with weight watchers you can join a community that knows exactly what you're going through and the leaders of the groups have just the right advice for most people. And if you can't afford to join a group - if you live too far or you don't have the time, then you can join the online community and get the support from the company itself.

The community or groups don't only provide support, but they also add to your sense of accomplishment. The group knows your progress and shares your excitement - even when you've only lost a few ounces - and this sense of accomplishment does wonders for your level of motivation. Because Weight Watchers has been around for so long, there is also tons of information about the diet. Recipes, meal plans and tips are easily found. You can even buy foods with weight watcher points marked on them.

One of the great things about Weight Watchers is the fact that there are no food restrictions. You are not told you can't have something, you are simply told to account for it in your points each day. The problem is, fueling your body with unhealthy options isn't going to give you the result you want. Yes, you may lose some weight, but your body will still feel sluggish and either hungry or bloated and uncomfortable. Using all points on burgers and fries every day isn't really changing your wellness mentality. You really must work to change the way you look at food and work to feed yourself better options more often than bad. Include some of your favorites on occasion, but focus on healthier things the bulk of the time.

Knowing how to do Weight Watchers for free will save you the expense of monthly meetings that you can turn over and pay for better healthier food options with instead.

HOW WEIGHT WATCHER BRING ABOUT WEIGHT LOSS

Weight Watchers is a weight loss program that relies on a point system for its recipes and foods, rather than enforcing a specific caloric restriction or other dietary restrictions, to help its followers achieve weight loss.

When you follow the Weight Watchers program, you are allowed to eat a certain number of "points" each day. Though some have criticized the program for relying on its own point number system rather than the actual calories, many people have found that it is easier to control how much food they eat when it is presented with an easier point number system like the Weight Watchers' SmartPoints. All food intakes must be controlled at all times, and calories must be accurately calculated. So for this practice to be effective, all members should have a Weight Watchers food scale, or a special kind of calculator that can keep track of your caloric intake.

To make Weight Watchers work, participants share their weight loss goals, eating habits, and activity preferences. The system then generates a daily point average. This average is found by considering how much weight participants want to lose and what the current body weight is. Every day the participants record the foods and quantities that they eat. These foods are assigned point values, and the goal of the participant is to remain within the average points that they are allowed for the day. This teaches participants to eat healthily and to come to an understanding of what they should avoid. For example, a cheeseburger may be 12 points. If a participant only has 20 points total for the day, then eating a cheeseburger will take up over half of their daily points. They can still eat the burger if they would like to, but in order to stick to the diet, they only have 8 points to use for all of the rest of their meals and snacks. But if that person instead had a cup of rice with a side of baked chicken and some spinach, they may only use 7 or 8 points, meaning that they can have more options for other meals. This teaches participants what foods are worse or better than others.

Those who sign up for weight watchers are also given a predetermined number of reserve points they can use whenever they would like. These points can be added to daily totals or can be saved until the end of every week.

WHAT IS SMARTPOINTS?

The SmartPoints plan makes healthy eating simple by putting complex nutritional information into one simple number. The Smart Points plan is based on the latest in nutritional science, nudging you toward a pattern, not only of weight loss, but of healthier eating with more fruits, vegetables and lean protein, and less sugar and saturated fat. SmartPoints values are generated from the calories, saturated fat, sugars and protein in food. The value is initially determined by the calories, then protein lowers the point value and saturated fat and sugars raise it. The final value is a balance of these factors.

Foods with higher amounts of sugar and saturated fats have higher SmartPoints values. Foods with higher amounts of lean protein have lower SmartPoints values. Many lean proteins like chicken and seafood are now lower in points and sweet treats like muffins, cookies and sugar sweetened beverages are higher. And about 40 percent of foods have stayed the same.

Smart Points will still help you lose unwanted pounds, but you may also experience having more energy and seeing your clothes fit better.

A food item can have the same value for calories and protein, but if the sugars or saturated fat are higher in one item versus the other, the point value will be higher. Giving each nutritional item different values in the calculation will help guide you to the healthier food item even though both have the same amount of calories.

HOW TO CALCULATE SMART POINTS EVERYDAY YOU NEED?

SmartPoints target is a number based on your gender, Age, Height and Weight.

Gender:

Female- score 2

Male- score 8

A nursing mom- score 12

Age

17-26- score 4

27-37- score 3

38-47- score 2

48-58- score 1

over 58- score 0

Weight

Enter the first one or two digits of your weight in pounds.

(For example, if you weigh 198 pounds, you will add 19 to your score; if you weigh 79 pounds, you will add 7 to your score)

Height

Under 5'1- score 0

5'1-5'10- score 1

Over 5'10- score 2

How do you spend most of your day?

Sitting down? Score 0

Occasional sitting? Score 2

Walking most of the time? Score 4

Doing physically hard work most of the time? Score 6

Just add all of your scores together and that's your daily point allowance.

Now that you know how many points you need to use each day, it's time to figure out what points are in your food. SmartPoints numbers in foods are assigned based on four components. These are calories, saturated fat, sugar, and protein. Protein lowers the amount of SmartPoints values while Sugar and saturated fat increase the SmartPoints values. So, healthier, lower-calorie foods cost fewer points. There is a very accurate calculator for this. Please check here.(http://www.calculator.net/weight-watchers-points-calculator.html)

As you lose weight, your SmartPoints number adjusts so you can continue to drop pounds. The point number that helps you lose weight initially may be too great when your body shrinks in size. A smaller body uses less energy, so it requires fewer points to continue to lose weight. When you reach your goal weight and switch to maintenance, your Weight Watchers SmartPoints target shifts slightly upwards to keep you from losing too much weight. This higher point value helps even out your energy balance, so you consume and expend relatively equal amounts to maintain your weight. Sustaining a successful weight loss requires you continue to make good food choices most of the time, though.

PROS AND CONS OF SMART POINTS

Pros

- Fruits and vegetables are considered "free foods" which is great for getting yourself to eat more fruits and veggies
- Flexibility to shape your own diet

- Weight loss at a steady rate is more likely to be maintained. But like with any program, consistency makes a big difference.
- Cooking at home is encouraged. You're more likely to eat healthy foods if you cook them yourself.

Cons

- You may need to cut out a lot of your prepackaged snacks and foods (even ones that are low calorie) as their point value can be way more than they would be if you were just counting calories.
- If you don't like counting calories, you may not like counting SmartPoints either.
- The ability to choose anything you want to eat may prove too tempting for some. It is completely possible to use all your SmartPoints on less-than-nutritious foods. For those dieters, weight loss plans that offer strict eating guidelines may work better.
- You may need to cut out a lot of your prepackaged snacks and foods (even ones that are low calorie) as their point value can be way more than they would be if you were just counting calories.

SHOULD I TAKE MORE EXERCISE?

Although you do not have to exercise to lose weight on Weight Watchers, the program acknowledges the importance of exercise and encourages you to integrate exercise into your weight loss routine. It's great for your health if you eat better and get moving.

Most of us seem to rely on exercise to help us slim down a lot more than we should. That could partly be because we view working out as the cruel tax we have to pay so we can eat that burger we really want.

SHOULD I CUT MY FOODS INTAKE?

If you are thinking about reducing your weight the first thing you need to think about doing is lowering your food intake. You know that your weight has increased because you have consumed more food than you actually need and the problem needs to be addressed with some urgency.

The simple solution therefore is to moderate the quantity of food you consume and your weight will disappear. This is in fact true but there is a snag. Simply cutting your food intake can leave you feeling hungry. For the majority of people this feeling of hunger is more than they can tolerate and they begin to let their diet slip. As a result they are unable to lose weight. Not eating is one of the worst things you can do. You will feel physically and emotionally unbalanced. You will crave bad food, your metabolism will slow down and your body will go into starvation mode holding onto fat stores. Eat small amounts and often.

ESSENTIAL TIPS OF WEIGHT WATCHERS DIET

- Keep A Journal - This is a definite must! There is no way to keep track of everything without one. You must update your journal with all the foods/drinks you consume on a daily basis. Most of the times we tend to forget those few snacks that we had throughout the day. By always having your journal handy, write it down immediately whether it be just a few cookies or just a glass of wine.

- Grocery Shopping - Make a list! And before you go grocery shopping, make sure you know the point values of the foods you buy before going to the supermarket. It's a good idea to write down the points values of the items you're going to by next to each item on your list. If something isn't on your list that you found in the supermarket, be sure to read those labels and serving sizes. Calculate those points!

- Use The Calculator - Make some informed decisions and use the SmartPoint calculator to figure out exactly how many points something is and don't just guess. Knowing how many points something is will help you make that decision if you think you are still hungry and want something more.

- Feel free to mix and match the meals depending on what you fancy.

- If you're hungry, you can snack on fruit and vegetables, which mostly contain 0 Points.

- It's important to drink at least six to eight glasses of fluids throughout the day. This can include coffee, tea, sugar-free squash, diet drinks and water.

- Simply eat three meals a day, and snack on fruit and vegetables which are mostly 0 Points.

- Use snacks with a low point value to prevent hunger throughout the day between meals.

- While you can have anything you want, it's healthier - and will use up fewer points - if you steer clear of typical high-fat, high-sodium snack foods and make nutritious choices.

CAUTIONS

Weight Watchers is not for children under age 10 or pregnant women. Children under age 17 must present written medical permission before they are allowed to partake. Anyone whose weight is within 5 lb (2.3 kg) of the lowest weight should not get on the program. You have to possess a common sense approach on the Weight Watchers program because you can eat what you want to. You could use all your points on chocolate if you want!!! But of course that would not be sensible. You have to be aware of what your body needs as a balance has to be struck. You need protein, calcium, carbohydrates for energy, plus assorted vitamin A and minerals.

Anyone who is under treatment for an illness, taking prescription drugs, or on a therapeutic diet (e.g. low sodium, gluten-free) should consult his/her doctor about the Weight Watchers plan and follow any changes or modifications the physician makes to the Weight.

FAQs

I don't like going to meetings, can't I just do it by myself?

Of course yes! Although the meetings are a huge part of the success but you can get as much success by yourself.

What are some of the best Weight Watcher recipes?

There are a lot of good Weight Watchers recipes out there. You just have to try them out to know which is best for you. Ready to get psyched for some tasty recipes that are easy on your waistline yet satisfying and full of flavor? Check out Weight Watcher recipes.

What advice do you have for someone starting Weight Watchers?

Make the time to plan out your week of food and go grocery shopping at the start of every week. Prep as much as you can in advance, too. If you have trouble with portion control, divide snacks into single portion-sizes in plastic baggies, or buy pre-portioned items.

Is SmartPoint Calculation easy?

Yes, it's easy and gets a lot easier to calculate once you've been on Weight Watcher for a while.

PART 2: WHY INSTANT POT?

KNOW ABOUT INSTANT POT

It's no surprise the Instant P0t is as popular as it is. People have fallen in love with their Instant Pots. They may like their blenders, cherish their slow cookers and need their food processors. But the Instant Pot - a device that combines an electric pressure cooker, slow cooker, rice cooker and yogurt maker in one handy unit - sends even mild-mannered cooks into fits of passion.

What makes Instant Pot different from the conventional kind that you would heat over a burner and then regulate yourself is that it is designed with a slew of self-regulating safety features, including sensors to monitor the unit's temperature and amount of pressure. All you do is plug it in and tap a button, and it does everything else. It's as user-friendly as a slow cooker - except that it gets dinner on the table a day or so faster.

If you're new to the slow cooker or pressure cooker, the Instant Pot is going to take some getting used to. There are so many buttons and settings to consider that it might feel overwhelming at first, but don't let that deter you.

BUTTONS AND FEATURES

There are 16-18 buttons on the Control Panel depending on which Instant Pot you have. But most Instant Pot Recipes are developed using 5 Buttons (Manual Button/ Pressure Cook, Adjust Button; Keep Warm/Cancel Button, Sauté function, "+" & "-" Buttons), because they give the control to cook precisely and accurately.

Sauté function- Use the Sauté button to sauté in the pressure cooking pot with the lid off. You can also press Sauté and the Adjust button once (more) for browning. Press Sauté and the Adjust button twice (less) to simmer.

Keep Warm/Cancel Button- Use this button to cancel a function or turn off your pressure cooker. On the Smart, you can use the Adjust button to reduce or increase the keep warm temperature from 145° (normal) to 133° (less) and 167° (more).

Manual button is an all purpose button. Use the manual button if a recipe says to pressure cook on high pressure for a specific number of minutes.

"+" and "-" buttons- Use to increase or decrease the cooking time.

Adjust Button- Press this to change from Normal Setting (default) to More Setting to Less Setting

*Note: for newer Instant Pot models with no "Adjust" Button – directly press the program buttons to scroll through the three functions (i.e. Press "Saute" button twice to go from Saute Normal to Saute More)

It may seem a little intimidating at first because of all the buttons, but really it's easy. Before you know it you'll be whipping up fabulous and nutritious meals.

USEFUL TIPS OF USING INSTANT POT

- **Use the Saute button for cooking as you would in a pan.**

Want to saute vegetables in the Instant Pot? You can do that and basically cook up anything as you would in a skillet or pan. You don't need the 1 cup of liquid. Just press the saute button, add some cooking oil or animal fat like beef tallow or lard to the inner pot and add food you want to cook like a skillet or pan. You can even adjust the saute temperature.

- **Adjust the temperature for certain functions.**

There are 3 adjustable temperatures for the Saute and Slow Cooker functions. Just use the Adjust button to increase or decrease the temperature. You can also adjust the cooking, time and pressure setting for the preset buttons (e.g. Bean/Chili or Rice).

- **Don't overdo the liquid.**

Because food cooks in a closed, sealed pot when cooking under pressure, you have less evaporation and should therefore use less cooking liquid than when cooking in a conventional pot. Regardless of what you're cooking, however, always use enough liquid. A good rule of thumb is at least 1 cup of liquid; however, check the owner's manual or the recipe to see exactly what the instant pot manufacturer recommends. Never fill the pot more than halfway with liquid.

- **Don't fill any instant pot with too much food.**

Never fill a instant pot more than two-thirds full with food. Also, never pack food tightly into a pressure cooker. If you don't follow these basic rules for cooking under pressure, the instant pot won't operate efficiently, affecting how the food comes out. You may also cause the safety valves to activate, especially if there's too much food in the pot.

- **Remember that even pieces mean evenly cooked food.**

Food should be cut into uniform-sized pieces so that they cook in the same amount of time.

- **Use stop-and-go cooking for perfect results.**

When making a recipe that contains ingredients that cook at different times, begin by partially cooking slow-to-cook foods, such as meat, first. Then use a quick-release method to stop the instant pot. Next, add the faster-cooking ingredients - such as green beans or peas - to the meat. Bring the pot back up to pressure again and finish everything up together at the same time..

- **Never open the Instant Pot while it's in Manual/Pressure mode.**

Once you close the lid and select the Manual/Pressure mode, make sure the pressure valve is set to Sealing. That will ensure the instant pot feature will work. You have 10 seconds to press the Cancel mode to stop cooking. After that, the instant pot is coming to pressure - and if you open the lid you'll be hit with a face full of steam. It's actually difficult to open the lid while it's cooking for that reason - that's why the instant pot is so intuitive. So once you close that lid, let it cook for the full time you've set.

- **Do pressure cooking the super-easy way.**

Choose the desired pressure level by pressing either the high or low pressure button on the control panel. Then, set the desired time you want to cook under pressure by pressing the high or low button for increasing or decreasing cook time. Now, press Start. The instant pot starts the countdown time when the level of pressure you chose is reached. It then beeps when done; telling you your food is ready.

- **Bear in mind that high altitude means longer cooking times.**

You may have to increase the cooking times if you live at an elevation of 3,000 feet above sea level or higher. A good general rule is to increase the cooking time by 5 percent for every 1,000 feet you are above the first 2,000 feet above sea level.

- **Release pressure when done.**

When the food is done cooking under pressure, use the appropriate pressure-release method, according to the recipe you're making.

There are 3 ways to open the Cooker that are a must-know:

- ✓ Quick Release: Release pressure instantly, by pressing 'Cancel' then twisting the steam release handle on the lid to the 'Venting' position.

✓ Natural Release: Continue cooking using the instant pot's residual heat and steam, by pressing 'Cancel' and waiting for the pressure to come down on its own and the lid to unlock…this will take about 20 minutes (longer if the cooker is very full)

✓ 10-minute Natural Release: Let the pot go into 'Keep Warm' mode and count 10 minutes. Then press 'Cancel' and twist the steam release handle on the lid to the 'Venting' position.

CAUTIONS IN USING INSTANT POT

Right off the bat we can get the safety issue out of the way. Most Instant Pots have built-in safety features, so as long as you follow directions and use common sense, you don't have to worry about kitchen explosions or getting injured while making meals.

Read the manual. There are a lot of important things in the manual so it's recommended that you thoroughly reading your manual before you get started.

It is hot. The Instant Pot gets hot. It does say "Caution" on it, so just remember that (especially if you have little hands working with you).

Double check the vent to make sure it's closed.

There is a little pin (red or silver, depending on your model) on the top of the Instant Pot that indicates whether the Instant Pot has come to pressure or not. You have to remember if the pin (float valve) was up or down when it wasn't at pressure. If you see steam coming out of the vent valve during cooking, or the pot is not coming to pressure or the silver button does not pop up, don't panic. You may see steam escaping during cooking until it comes to pressure. This is normal. The silver button will pop up when it reaches pressure but if the pot does not reach pressure and you don't see the silver button pop up. it may be due to the fact that:

1. You are not cooking enough food, like 1 cup of rice.

2. If the ring is loose and the lid is not sealing completely.

If (1) happens, don't worry. The pot is still hot and your food is still being cooked. Just open the pot and check it. If not cooked, close the lid and try again with less time. (2) can happen if you use the pot to make food for too long. (i.e. two batches of bone broth as 120 minutes each batch.) If the ring stays heated for a very long time under pressure, it'll stretch out and not fit the lid properly. So you have to shrink the ring by running it under cold water or putting it in the fridge before using it.

WHERE TO BUY GOOD INSTANT POT

The Instant Pot comes in Lux, Duo, or Smart models. The Lux boasts 6 functions (Pressure Cooker, Sauté/Browning, Slow Cooker, Rice Cooker, Steamer, and Warmer). It lacks both the yogurt function and its pressure cooking function offers only high (not high and low). The Duo boasts 7 functions (Pressure Cooker, Slow Cooker, Rice Cooker, Sauté/Browning, Yogurt Maker, Steamer, and Warmer) - all the ones that the Lux has plus the yogurt setting. Additionally, its pressure cooking setting allows you to choose low or high. The low pressure is handy with more delicate foods.

The Smart model has the 7 functions of the Duo, plus additional downloadable recipe programs and 3 temperature choices on the Keep Warm function. The main draw on this model is the "smart" bluetooth functionality that allows you to run it from your phone or tablet. It has other things as part of the "smart" features, too.

It's always worth checking prices of the Instant Pot before deciding where to buy as there are many sales channels on the internet and retail locations offering a wide variety of models. The majority of good Instant Pots are sold on Amazon.

HOW TO MAINTAIN IT

Maintaining your Instant Pot can be surprisingly tricky, especially when cooking with stinky food. Keep in mind that you should never submerge the electronic base into water - only spot clean this. However, the stainless steel pot and the interior of the lid can be washed and cleaned. First, make sure your machine is unplugged! That may seem a little silly to say…but you just never know! Second, remove the pot and the lid from the base, as you will clean these separately. Hand wash the lid with warm soap and water. Typically, the lid doesn't get too dirty with food (unless you are dripping things on it), so it doesn't usually need deeper cleaning than that. Then, remove the steam-release handle and the anti-block shield (following instructions in your manual) to clean out any particles that may have gone into there.

You can hand wash the stainless steel pot by hand or in the dishwasher. Using vinegar can help get rid of any particularly pungent smells that have stuck around. Keep your Instant Pot in a cool and dry place.

FAQs

What is an Instant Pot? Is it the same as a pressure cooker?

Yes, Instant Pot is currently one of the most popular electric pressure cooker brands. It is a multi-functional cooker that has some extra functions compare to traditional stove-top pressure cookers.

Is it easy to cook with an Instant Pot?

There's a learning curve to cook with pressure cookers. But no worries! Once you're familiar with it, you will find the cooking relatively easy.

Which Instant Pot is best for me?

The pressure multi cookers all pressure cook, slow cook and saute'. They all also have a "manual" program, this is important because it means you can tap in your own pressure cooking time and pressure, (if available). All of the Instant Pots with pressure function come with a stainless-steel cooking surface and, most importantly, the same safety features.

Are there any disadvantages with cooking in the Instant Pot?

One disadvantage about cooking with Instant Pot is you can't inspect, taste, or adjust the food along the way. That's why it's essential to follow recipes with accurate cooking times.

Is Instant Pot safe to use?

Modern day electric pressure cookers such as the Instant Pot are quiet, very safe and easy to use.

Which size Instant Pot should I buy?

First of all, keep in mind that as with any pot that's advertised as holding a certain volume; you cannot use all of it. Who fills a pot to the top? If you're pressure cooking in the Instant Pot, you cannot overfill it or you'll have a problem. The max fill line is a little more than 3/4 full. So when you're choosing your Instant Pot, choose a higher volume capacity than you think you need. You probably won't regret bigger, but you certainly will regret too small.

My Instant Pot recently started making clicking noises while it's cooking. Do I need to worry?

There are two reasons for clicking sounds while the Instant Pot is operational. One is that the inner pot is wet on the outside. Make sure the Instant Pot inner pot is dry before you put it in the Instant Pot unit. The second reason for the clicking sounds is that the Instant Pot is internally regulating power through power switching. This is perfectly normal and you don't need to worry.

My Instant Pot is not reaching pressure and my float valve is not sealing. How can I troubleshoot this problem?

Two of the most common reasons why your float valve is not popping up: the sealing ring is installed improperly or there isn't enough liquid to bring the Instant Pot to pressure. Although there are many more reasons an Instant Pot won't pressurize.

Can I use the Instant Pot for Pressure Frying?

Don't attempt to pressure fry in any electric pressure cookers. The splattering oil may melt the gasket. KFC uses a commercial pressure fryer (modern ones operate at 5 PSI) specially made to fry chickens.

What kind of accessories or containers can I use in the Instant Pot?

You can use any oven-safe accessories and containers. Remember that different materials will conduct heat differently so cooking times may vary. Stainless steel containers are highly recommended as they conduct heat quickly.

PART 3: 101 WEIGHT WATCHERS INSTANT POT RECIPES

Breakfast

1: Brown Butter Oatmeal

Serves: 5 people   **Preparation time:** 5 mins   **Cooking Time:** 17 mins
Smart Points: 3

Ingredients:

1. 2 tablespoons of unsalted butter
2. 1 ½ cups of oats, steel cut
3. 4 ½ cups of warm water
4. ½ teaspoon of salt, can change according to taste
5. Brown sugar, for serving
6. Heavy Cream, for serving

Directions:

1. Press the sauté mode on your Instant Pot, and melt the butter. Add the oats into the pot and heat it for 5 minutes whilst still stirring until the oats are lightly roasted.
2. Add the water, salt and continue stirring. Make sure that all the ingredients are submerged into the water. If not, then add more.
3. Close the lid and adjust the 'Steam release' to 'sealing'. Change the cooking mode to 'Porridge' and cook it for 12 minutes at a high pressure.
4. When the cooking stops, let the pressure release naturally, and after 10 minutes, set the 'Steam Release' back to 'venting' to remove the remaining steam.
5. Take the oatmeal out of the pot and ladle it into a bowl. Serve it with the brown sugar and heavy cream. You can also try variations with various other ingredients, like peanut butter, sesame soy and blueberry almond. Enjoy!

2: Apple and Cinnamon Oatmeal

Serves: 4 people

Preparation time: 5 minutes

Cooking Time: 9 minutes

Smart Points: 4

Ingredients:

1. 3 tablespoons of regular butter
2. 1 cup of steel cut oats
3. 2 ½ cups of water
4. 1 large apple, chopped, cored and peeled. More to be needed for garnishing
5. 1 tablespoon of brown sugar, for serving
6. 1 teaspoon of cinnamon
7. ½ teaspoon of salt, more or less depending on your taste

Directions:

1. Select the sauté function of the Instant Pot and let it preheat. When the display indicator reads hot, add the butter and oats, and cook for 2 minutes.
2. Add the water, chopped apple, brown sugar, salt and cinnamon and stir well.
3. Secure the lid, set the setting to 'manual' and cook at high pressure for 7-9 minutes, depending on the amount of thickness you want.
4. Once the cooking is complete, let the steam release itself, and after 10 minutes, release the remaining steam by setting the 'Steam Release' setting to 'venting'.
5. Serve the oatmeal with brown sugar and nicely topped fresh apple. Enjoy!

3: Easy-to-make Vanilla Yogurt

Serves: 6 people

Preparation time: 10 minutes

Cooking Time: 10 hours, 15 minutes

Smart Points: 5

Ingredients:

1. 4 cups of milk, 2% fat
2. 100 grams' vanilla yogurt, or a small container equivalent
3. 1 tablespoons of sugar
4. 4 cups of water

Directions:

1. Boil the milk on a high heat using a non-stick pot, or through the sauté option on the Instant Pot.
2. Let the milk cool at the room temperature.
3. After the milk has cooled down, add the yogurt, sugar and divide the mix into 4 different cups. If you used the Instant Pot in this step, clean it for the next one).
4. Add the water to the 4 cup mark in the Instant Pot and put all the four cups in the pot again. This is to ensure that the water level is equal to the amount of milk.
5. Secure the lid and choose the 'Keep warm' function for 15 minutes.
6. Let the pot rest in the warm heat for 10 hours. Do not open the lid, or all will go to waste.
7. After 10 hours has elapsed, take the yogurt out, cover it with a plastic wrap and let it chill for 2-3 hours before serving. Enjoy!

4: Classical Irish Oatmeal

Serves: 4-6 people

Preparation time: 15 minutes

Cooking Time: 13 minutes

Smart Points: 3

Ingredients:

1. ½ teaspoon of salt
2. 2 tablespoons of butter
3. 1 cup of steel-cut oats
4. 3 cups of water
5. ½ teaspoon of grounded cinnamon
6. ½ teaspoon of salt
7. ¼ cup of half-and-half, a common product found at dairy stores.
8. ¼ brown sugar
9. 1 cup of strawberries, for berry compote
10. 6 ounces of blackberries, for berry compote
11. 6 ounces of blueberries, for berry compote
12. 1 tablespoons of water, for berry compote
13. 3 tablespoons of sugar, granulated, for berry compote

Directions:

To make oatmeal:

1. Select the sauté function on the Instant Pot, and melt the butter. Add the oats and cook for 5 minutes while still stirring continuously.
2. Add the water, cinnamon, salt, and cook for 1 minute.
3. Close the lid, and cook at a high pressure for 13 minutes. Don't forget to set the 'Steam release' to 'Sealing'.

4. While the oatmeal is cooking, it would be the best time to make the berry compote. If you want to, you can, but you can also leave it for the end, as it is optional.
5. When the cooking is complete, naturally let the steam release and after 10 minutes, release the remaining pressure. Stir the oat until it is smooth.
6. Add half brown sugar, and stir till there are no lumps and the mix is perfectly blended.
7. Serve with Berry Compote. If you want the porridge to be thicker, cook the oatmeal for 2-3 minutes more at the sauté mode.

To make the Compote:

1. Mix the strawberries, blackberries, blueberries, water, sugar in a saucepan and simmer it using a medium heat.
2. Cook it for 8 to 9 minutes or until the berries are soft enough. Thereafter, serve it with the Oatmeal. Enjoy!

5: Peaches and Cream Oatmeal

Serves: 4 people

Prep Time: 5 minutes

Cooking Time: 3 minutes

Smart Points: 4

Ingredients:

1. 3 cups of oats, any types to taste
2. 4 cups of warm water
3. 1 peach, finely chopped
4. 1 teaspoon of vanilla
5. 2 tablespoons of flax meal, optional
6. 1/2 cup of Almonds, chopped into small pieces, optional
7. Milk, optional. Can also use cream if desired.
8. Maple Syrup, for additional taste, optional

Directions:

1. Add the rolled oats, peaches, vanilla and water into the Instant Pot. Adjust the mode to 'porridge' and cook at a high pressure for 3 minutes.
2. When finished, allow the heat and pressure to manually release itself, then after 10 minutes, remove the remaining by doing a quick pressure release.
3. Divide the porridge between 3 to 4 bowls, and serve it with the optional ingredients stated in the list above. Enjoy!

6: Purple Yam Barley Porridge

Serves: 12 people

Prep Time: 10 minutes

Cooking Time: 45 minutes

Smart Points: 4

Ingredients:

1. 3 tablespoons of pot barley
2. 3 tablespoons of pearl barley
3. 3 tablespoons of buckwheat
4. 3 tablespoons of black eye beans
5. 3 tablespoons of glutinous rice
6. 3 tablespoons of black glutinous rice
7. 3 tablespoons of Romano beans
8. 3 tablespoons of red beans
9. 3 tablespoons of brown rice
10. 1 purple yam, about 300 gms
11. 1/6 teaspoon of baking soda, optional

Directions:

1. Clean the purple yam, remove the skin and cut it into 1 centimeter cubes. Wash the barley, rice and beans as well.
2. Put the yam, rice, barley, beans and baking soda into the Instant Pot and add the water up to the 8 cups mark in the inner pot.
3. Secure the lid and set the mode to 'Manual'. Let the mix cook for 45 minutes.
4. When the time is up, let the pot sit for 10 minutes, then release the pressure. Serve and enjoy!

7: Maple French Toast Casserole

Serves: 8 people

Prep Time: 8 minutes

Cooking Time: 1 hour, 30 minutes

Smart Points: 5

Ingredients:

1. Cooking Spray, so that the ingredients don't stick in the Instant Pot.
2. 12 slices of sandwich bread cut into small 1 inch pieces. Can also use gluten-free bread if desired
3. 4 eggs, lightly beaten
4. 1/2 cup of maple syrup
5. 1 teaspoon of cinnamon
6. 1/2 teaspoon of kosher salt
7. 1/4 teaspoon of nutmeg, grated
8. 1/8 teaspoon of cloves
9. 2 cups of milk, reduced fat 2%
10. 1 teaspoon of powdered sugar

Directions:

1. Coat the inner pot of the Instant pot with the cooking spray. And place the cubed bread in the pot.
2. Mix the eggs, cinnamon, cloves, salt, nutmeg, and maple syrup in a large bowl. Add the milk and whisk all the ingredients till they are well blended.
3. Transfer the mix on the bread into the Instant Pot with a spoon, and then gently press the mixture so that all bread pieces are coated.
4. Secure the lid of the pot, select the 'Slow Cook' mode and set the time to 90 minutes.
5. After the time is up, serve with a sprinkle of powdered sugar. Enjoy!

8: Pink Lady Applesauce

Serves: 8 to 10 people

Prep Time: 15 minutes

Cooking Time: 25 minutes

Smart Points: 4

Ingredients:

1. 12 apples
2. 1 cup ofwarm or cold water
3. 2 tablespoons of zesty lemon juice

Directions:

1. Cut the apples into quarters, and peel them if you desire to. Add them to the Instant Pot along with the water and lemon juice.
2. Secure the lid and set the mode to 'Manual', and cook for 5 minutes.
3. When the timer sounds, let the Instant Pot rest for 10 to 15 minutes, then take the sauce out. If you want a thicker texture, then use a blender till you reach the desired result.
4. Place the sauce in jars into the fridge, and re-heat it whenever you want to! Enjoy!

9: Soy Milk Yogurt

Serves: 4 to 6 people

Prep Time: 15 minutes

Cooking Time: 14 hours

Smart Points: 5

Ingredients:

1. 3/4 cup of powdered soy milk
2. 1 teaspoon of sugar
3. 2 1/2 cups of hot water
4. 3/4 teaspoon of agar powder
5. 1/4 teaspoon of probiotic or vegan culture

Directions:

1. Add the water, soy milk, sugar into a blender and blend at a high speed for 3 minutes.
2. Add the agar powder into the mix and blend it also for 30 more seconds. After blending, allow the soy milk to settle down for 2-5 minutes.
3. Once the soy milk has settled down, add the probiotic powder or vegan culture and WHISK (don't blend)
4. Place the mixture into the Instant Pot, select the 'Yogurt' mode and set the timer to 14 hours,then wait.
5. Once the time is up, take the yogurt out and let it sit in the refrigerator for 2 more hours. You can skip this if you want to use it immediately. Enjoy!

10: Slow-Cook Oatmeal with Apples

Serves: 10 people

Prep Time: 3 minutes

Cooking Time: 6 hours

Smart Points: 5

Ingredients:

1. 1 pound of apples, diced
2. 2 cups of steel cut oats
3. 7 cups of water
4. 1/2 cup of honey, or maple syrup for vegans
5. 1/2 teaspoon of salt
6. 1/2 teaspoon of all-spice, grounded
7. 1 can coconut of milk, light
8. toasted cashews, optional
9. more apples, for topping, optional

Directions:

1. Cover the inner pot of the Instant Pot with oil and add the first seven ingredients in the inner pot.
2. Secure the lid, set the mode to 'Slow Cook', adjust it to 'Less' and cook for 6 hours.
3. Stir well before serving and garnish with cashews and apples, if desired. Enjoy!

11: Three minute Oats

Serves: 4 people

Prep Time: 2 minutes

Cooking Time: 3 minutes

Smart Points: 5

Ingredients:

1. 2 cups of warm water
2. 1 cup of milk, can be dairy, almond variations
3. 1 cup of steel cut oats
4. 1/2 vanilla bean
5. a pinch of salt
6. 1/2 cup of raisins or any other dry fruit
7. 1 teaspoon of cinnamon, grounded
8. 1/4 cup of walnuts
9. 1/2 tablespoon of maple syrup
10. olive oil, optional
11. 1 cinnamon stick, optional

Directions:

1. Add the water, milk, oats, vanilla bean, salt, cinnamon stick, olive oil and 1/4 cup of raisins to the Instant Pot.
2. Secure the lid, set the mode to 'Manual' and cook for 3 minutes. When the time is up, let the pressure come down itself.
3. Open the pot to check if the oats are cooked properly, if not, secure the lid again and let it rest for 10 minutes.
4. Once the oats are cooked, remove the vanilla bean, cinnamon stick and set it aside.
5. Stir the cinnamon, walnuts and the remaining raisins and sweetener for taste. You can refrigerate leftovers for up to 4 days, so enjoy!

Dessert

12: Basic Rice Pudding

Serves: 4 people

Prep Time: 5 minutes

Cooking Time: 15 minutes

Smart Points: 3

Ingredients:

1. 1 cup of fine rice
2. 1 teaspoon of butter
3. 2 cups of non fat milk
4. 3/4 cups of sugar
5. 1 cup of water
6. 2 egg yolks
7. 1/2 cup of half-and-half
8. 1 tablespoon of vanilla
9. 1 teaspoon of cinnamon, optional
10. 1/4 cup of raisins, optional

Directions:

1. Set the Instant Pot mode to 'sauté'. Melt the butter, and then add the rice. Cook it for about 3 minutes, until the edges of the rice become golden.
2. While the rice is cooking, whisk the milk, water, sugar and when the rice gets cooked, add them to the Instant Pot.
3. Set the mode to 'Manual' and cook at a high pressure for 10 minutes. After the time gets exhausted, let the pressure release itself, then do a quick release.
4. While the pressure is releasing, whisk the eggs, vanilla and the half-and-half.

5. Once you open the pot, add half a cup of the rice mixture into the egg mix, stirring constantly. Pour the resultant mixture back into the Instant Pot with the optional ingredients.
6. Set the mode back to 'sauté' and cook for 3 minutes while constantly stirring the mixture.
7. Then serve either warm or cold, according to your preference. Enjoy!

13: Quick Apple Pie Rice Pudding

Serves: 4 people

Prep Time: 5 minutes

Cooking Time: 5 minutes

Smart Points: 4

Ingredients:

1. 4 cups of rice, preferably grain brown
2. 4 cups of apples, finely chopped into small cubes
3. 2 cups of non-dairy, unsweetened milk
4. 1 tablespoon of Apple Pie Spice, or cinnamon, whichever you prefer
5. 1 tablespoon of Vanilla
6. 1/4 teaspoon of ground cardamom
7. 1 cup of golden raisins

Directions:

1. Place all the ingredients in the Instant Pot, and cook on a 'manual' mode for 5 minutes.
2. Once done, wait for the pressure to release itself slowly, and after 10 minutes, do a quick release.
3. Enjoy! Also, you can use this as a replacement for your usual oatmeal, and can serve it hot, cold or warm!

14: Carrot Pudding

Serves: 4 people

Prep Time: 10 minutes

Cooking Time: 20 minutes

Smart Points: 5

Ingredients:

1. 2 tablespoons of ghee, or vegan
2. 10 cups of carrots, grated and peeled
3. 1 cup of almond milk, unsweetened
4. 3/4 cup of sugar
5. 1 cup of almond meal
6. 2 teaspoons of cardamom powder
7. 2 tablespoons of raisins
8. 1/2 teaspoon of saffron
9. 2 tablespoon of pistachios, sliced

Directions:

1. Turn the Instant Pot on into the 'Sauté' mode, add the ghee and carrots. Cook for 2-3 minutes with the lid on.
2. Add the almond milk and close the lid, while making sure that the 'Pressure value' is set to 'sealing'.Thereafter set the Instant Pot to cook on 'Manual' and adjust to a high pressure for 5 minutes.
3. Quick release the pressure when the time is up, add the sugar, almond meal, raisins, saffron and cardamom powder. Mix all the ingredients well.
4. Turn the Instant Pot to 'Sauté' on a high heat again and cook for 5-7 minutes, until all the liquids are evaporated.
5. Garnish it with the sliced pistachios, serve and Enjoy!

15: Cheesecake Pops

Serves: 6 people, 18 pops

Prep Time: 30 minutes

Cooking Time: 30 minutes

Smart Points: 6

Ingredients:

1. 1/2 cup of sugar
2. 16 ounces' cream cheese, room temp.
3. 2 tablespoons of sour cream
4. 2 eggs
5. 1 teaspoon of vanilla extract
6. 1-pound of chocolate

Directions:

1. Using a mixing bowl, mix the cream cheese and sugar until it gets smooth. Blend in the sour cream ,vanilla and mix the eggs one at a time. Don't over mix tho.
2. Prepare a spring form the pan by coating it with non-stick spray. Transfer the batter prepared above into it.
3. Pour 1 cup of water into the Instant Pot, transfer the mixture and pan into the Instant Pot. Close the lid, select the 'High Pressure' and cook for 30 minutes. After the time has elapsed, use the quick release to remove the pressure.
4. Use a paper towel to soak up any pressure resultant water above the cheesecake, and remove the pan on a wire rack to cool. After it is cooled, refrigerate it for 4 hours or overnight while covering it with a plastic wrap.
5. After it is chilled, scoop the cake into small balls and insert a lollipop stick into each ball. Thereafter freeze it for 2 hours or more.
6. After the pops are frozen, dippen them into the melted chocolate. Shake off any excess, and refrigerate the pops until they are hard but easy to eat.

16: Cinnamon Raisin Bread Pudding

Serves: 6 to 8 people

Prep Time: 25 minutes

Cooking Time: 35 minutes

Smart Points: 5

Ingredients:

1. 4 to 5 cups of French Bread, cut to 1 inch cubes
2. 1 cup of raisins
3. 2 cups of milk
4. 2 eggs
5. 1 egg yolk
6. 1/4 cup of granulated sugar
7. 1/8 teaspoon of ground cinnamon
8. 1/8 teaspoon of ground nutmeg
9. 1 1/2 cup of water

Directions:

1. Spray a 7 inch round baking dish that fits in the Instant Pot with non-stick cooking spray. Mix the bread cubes and raisins in the dish, then distribute the raisins evenly.
2. Whisk the eggs, yolk, sugar, milk, nutmeg and cinnamon in a bowl until it is properly blended. Pour this mixture over the bread, and cover it with an aluminum foil. Thereafter, let it rest for 15 minutes.
3. Pour the water into the Instant Pot, place the baking dish inside and don't take off the foil.
4. Close the lid and cook for 35 minutes at the 'Manual' mode on a high pressure. When the cooking is complete, remove the pressure after 10 minutes.
5. Take the dish out, remove the foil, serve the pudding warm and enjoy!

17: Creamy Rice Pudding

Serves: 8 people

Prep Time: 10 minutes

Cooking Time: 16 minutes

Smart Points: 5

Ingredients:

1. 3/4 cup of sugar
2. 1/2 teaspoon of salt
3. 2 eggs
4. 5 cups of milk, 1% fat
5. 1 1/2 cups of Arborio or regular rice
6. 1 cup of half-and-half
7. 1 1/2 teaspoons of vanilla extract

Directions:

1. Mix the sugar, salt, rice and milk in the Instant Pot. Select the 'Sauté' mode and cook the contents uncovered till they are boiled. As soon as they start boiling, cover the lid.
2. Change the mode to 'Manual', adjust to a low pressure and cook for 16 minutes.
3. Whilst the rice is cooking, whisk the eggs, vanilla and the half-and-half. When the cooking is done, turn off the pressure cooker, and wait for 10 minutes before using the quick pressure release.
4. Add the egg mixture into the pot while stirring the rice, select the 'Sauté' mode and then cook it uncovered until the mixture boils.
5. Turn off the cooker, transfer the pudding into the bowls and serve immediately, or let them chill, your choice! Enjoy!

18: Crème Brulee

Serves: 6 to 10 people

Prep Time: 35 minutes

Cooking Time: 15 minutes

Smart Points: 6

Ingredients:

1. 2 cups of fresh cream
2. 5 tablespoons of white sugar
3. 6 egg yolks
4. 1 teaspoon of vanilla extract
5. 4 tablespoons of raw sugar, to be used for caramelizing

Directions:

1. Combine the egg yolks, sugar, cream and vanilla in a mixing bowl, then whisk until everything is combined properly, don't over mix tho.
2. Pour the mixture into the ramekins through a strainer, and cover them tightly in the foil. Put the ramekins into the Instant Pot, making sure they are vertically straight.
3. Cover the lid, and cook on the 'Manual' mode for 9 minutes. When the time is up, open the cooker using a natural release.
4. Take out the custards, and check by jiggling them. If they are almost solid in nature,it means they're OK, but if they feel watery, then cook for 5 more minutes.
5. Let the custards cool off for 30 minutes to an hour. Once they are cooled, put them in a refrigerator, and let them chill for 4 hours or overnight.
6. Before serving, sprinkle some raw sugar on top, then use a culinary torch or place them under the boiler for 5 minutes to caramelize. Enjoy!

19: One Step Arroz Pina Colada

Serves: 6 to 10 people

Prep Time: 5 minutes

Cooking Time: 15 minutes

Smart Points: 5

Ingredients:

1. 1 cup of Arborio rice
2. 1 cup of condensed milk, can add more for extra sweetness
3. 2/3 cup of pineapple juice
4. 1 ½ cups of water
5. 1 tablespoon of cinnamon
6. 1 cup of coconut milk, full fat

Directions:

1. Combine the rice and water in the Instant Pot, then cook at a low pressure for 12 minutes using either the 'rice' mode or the 'manual' mode.
2. When the cooking is dome, release the pressure quickly and add half of the coconut milk, all the condensed milk, the cinnamon and the pineapple juice. Thereafter, mix properly.
3. Let the mixture cool and absorb all the liquid. After it has thickened, add the remaining coconut milk to make the pudding thinner and Enjoy!

20: Pine Nuts Honey Mousse

Serves: 6 to 8 people

Prep Time: 15 minutes

Cooking Time: 25 minutes

Smart Points: 6

Ingredients:

1. 2 eggs
2. ½ cup of honey
3. 1 ¼ cup of coconut cream
4. 1 tablespoon of coconut oil
5. 1 ¼ cup of pine nuts
6. Chocolate Ganache, for topping

Directions:

1. Prepare a spring form pan by coating it with coconut oil, thereafter, line the bottom and sides with a parchment paper.
2. Put the eggs, honey and cream into a blender and mix until it gets completely smooth, then pour the mixture into the pan.
3. Pour one cup of water into the Instant Pot and place the pan inside. Close the lid and cook on a high pressure for 25 minutes using the 'Manual' mode.
4. Once the time is up, open the lid and take out the pan. Let it rest for 30 minutes or so. After that, invert the contents, take out the parchment paper, then put them again in the spring form pan, and let it refrigerate overnight.
5. If desired, top it with the Chocolate Ganache, or eat it without it. Enjoy!

21: Pressure Cooker Baked Apples

Serves: 6 apples

Prep Time: 5 minutes

Cooking Time: 20 minutes

Smart Points: 2

Ingredients:

1. 6 apples, cored
2. ¼ cup of raisins
3. 1 cup of red wine
4. ½ cup of sugar
5. 1 teaspoon of cinnamon

Directions:

1. Add the apples into the Instant Pot, and then sprinkle the raisins, sugar and cinnamon on top of it. Finally, add the red wine.
2. Cover the lid and cook on a high pressure for 10 minutes. When the time is up, let the pressure naturally release itself.
3. After the pressure has been released, serve it in a small bowl with lots of cooking liquid. Enjoy!

22: Red Wine Poached Pears

Serves: 6 people

Prep Time: 5 minutes

Cooking Time: 10 minutes

Smart Points: 5

Ingredients:

1. 6 pears, peeled
2. 1 bottle of red wine
3. 1 bay leaf
4. 1 stick of cinnamon
5. 4 cloves
6. 1-piece of ginger, fresh
7. 1 1/3 cups of sugar

Directions:

1. Pour the wine, bay leaf, cloves, ginger, sugar, cinnamon and pears into the Instant Pot.
2. Cover the lid and cook on a high pressure for 9 minutes using the 'Manual' mode. When the time is up, use the quick pressure release.
3. Take the pears out and cook the remaining liquid on the 'Sauté' mode until the volume of the liquid is reduced to at least half.
4. Take the liquid out, and pour it on the pears using a large bowl. Garnish it with preferred herbs and serve at a room temperature or chilled. Enjoy!

Poultry

23: BBQ Chicken Drumsticks

Serves: 4 to 6 people

Prep Time: 5 minutes

Cooking Time: 25 minutes

Smart Points: 6

Ingredients:

1. 4-10 chicken drumsticks
2. 4 ½ teaspoons of black pepper,
3. ¼ cup of sweet paprika
4. 1 tablespoon of salt
5. 1 ½ teaspoons of garlic powder
6. 1 ½ teaspoons of regular salt
7. 1 ½ teaspoons of cayenne pepper
8. 1 ½ teaspoons of dry mustard
9. 1 ½ teaspoons of ground cumin

Directions:

1. Add ¾ of cup of water into the Instant Pot, place the chicken drumsticks inside it, and cook it for 20 minutes using the 'Poultry' mode.
2. Preheat the oven and line a cookie sheet with some parchment paper. When the timer for the Instant Pot beeps open the lid and take out the drumsticks.
3. Coat the drumsticks with the BBQ rub evenly, and line them on the cookie sheet. Broil the drumsticks for 2 minutes per side, but be careful not to burn them.
4. Serve immediately. Enjoy!

24: Chicken Lazone

Serves: 6 people

Prep Time: 10 minutes

Cooking Time: 3 minutes

Smart Points: 7

Ingredients:

1. 2 teaspoons of garlic powder
2. 1 teaspoon of chili powder
3. 1 teaspoon of paprika
4. 1 teaspoon of onion powder
5. 1/2 teaspoon of pepper
6. 1 teaspoon of salt
7. 2 tablespoons of butter
8. 2-pound of tender chicken
9. 2 tablespoons of oil
10. 2 tablespoons of cornstarch
11. 1/2 cup of chicken broth
12. 2 cups of heavy cream
13. 2 tablespoons of water
14. 2 tablespoons of parsley, finely chopped
15. 12 ounces' of spaghetti, cooked through the package instructions

Directions:

1. Mix the garlic, onion, chicken powder, paprika, salt and pepper in a mixing bowl. Add the chicken and toss it with your hands to coat it completely with the spices.
2. Select the 'Sauté' mode and preheat the Instant Pot. When the pot gets hot, add the butter and oil and stir until the butter is completely melted. Add the chicken a few pieces at a time and sauté them on both sides.
3. When all the chicken has been sautéed, add the chicken broth to the pot. Secure

the lid and cook on high pressure for 3 minutes using the 'Manual' mode. When the time is up, do a quick release of the pressure.

4. In a small bowl, dissolve cornstarch in water. Add it to the pot, and stir to combine. Mix well.

5. Select the 'Sauté' mode again and stir until the sauce thickens. Take the sauce and chicken out and stir in heavy cream. Serve with spaghetti sprinkled with parsley. Enjoy!

25: Cola Chicken Wings

Serves: 2 to 4 people

Prep Time: 5 minutes

Cooking Time: 25 minutes

Smart Points: 7

Ingredients:

1. 1 1/2 pounds' of chicken wings
2. 1 stalk green onion, 2 inch pieces
3. 4 cloves of garlic, crushed finely
4. 1 tablespoon of ginger
5. 200 mL Coca Cola
6. 1 tablespoon of dark soy sauce
7. 2 tablespoons of light soy sauce
8. 1 tablespoon of peanut oil
9. 1 tablespoon of Chinese rice wine

Directions:

1. Preheat the Instant Pot and set the mode to 'Sauté'. Add the peanut oil, garlic, ginger and green onions into the pot, then let it cook for a minute. Add the chicken wings and stir for roughly one to two minutes.
2. When the edges of the chicken start getting brown, add the sauces, wine and mix properly. Thereafter cover the lid and cook on a high pressure for 5 minutes using the 'Manual' mode.
3. When the time is up, let the pressure naturally release itself. Taste the wings, sauce, then add more seasoning sauce and salt if required. Serve immediately with rice or other dishes. Enjoy!

26: Cranberry Braised Turkey Wings

Serves: 6 to 8 people

Prep Time: 10 minutes   **Cooking Time:** 25 minutes

Smart Points: 8

Ingredients:

1. 2 tablespoons of oil
2. 2 tablespoons of butter
3. 4 turkey wings, 2 to 3 pounds
4. salt, according to taste
5. pepper, according to taste
6. 1 cup of dried cranberries, soaked in water
7. 1 onion, sliced
8. 1 cup of orange juice
9. 1 cup of walnuts
10. 1 cup of vegetable stock
11. 1 bunch thyme

Directions:

1. Preheat the Instant Pot using the 'Sauté' function, then melt the butter and add the olive oil. Place the turkey wings in the Instant Pot and make it brownish on both sides, adding the salt and pepper to taste.
2. Remove the wings when browned and add the onions, followed by the wings again with the brown side facing upwards. Then add the cranberries, walnuts,thyme and pour the orange juice/stock in the pot as well.
3. Cover the lid, and then cook for 20 minutes on a high pressure using the 'Manual' mode. When the time is up, remove the thyme and move the wings to a serving dish.
4. Place the wings to a broiler for 5 minutes, and when the wings caramelize, reduce the remaining contents by half using the 'Sauté' mode.
5. Pour the liquid over the wings and Enjoy!

27: Easy BBQ Chicken Thighs

Serves: 4 people   **Prep Time:** 5 mins   **Cooking Time:** 30 mins   **Smart Points:** 7

Ingredients:

1. 1 teaspoon of olive oil
2. 1 medium sized onion, sliced
3. 2 pounds' of chicken, skinless
4. 1 cup of barbeque sauce
5. 1/4 cup of honey
6. 1/2 cup of ketchup
7. 1/2 teaspoon of black pepper
8. 1 teaspoon of salt
9. 1/4 teaspoon of cumin
10. 1/4 teaspoon of onion powder
11. 1/4 teaspoon of garlic powder
12. ¼ teaspoon of smoked paprika
13. 1/4 teaspoon of paprika
14. pinch chili flakes

Directions:

1. Preheat the Instant Pot using the 'Sauté' option and add the oil. When it is heated, add the chicken and brown each side for 3 minutes. While the chicken is browning, mix the remaining ingredients in a mixing bowl.
2. Spread the onion around the chicken and cover it with the sauce. Cook on a high pressure for 10 minutes using the 'Manual' mode.
3. While the chicken is cooking, line a sheet pan with the foil and set the broiler to a high pressure. When the chicken is done, remove the chicken with thetongs (as it will be falling apart) and place it under the broiler for 3 minutes on each side.
4. While the chicken is browning, switch to the 'Sauté' mode and cook until the sauce has reduced to about half the volume. Once done, pour it over on the browned chicken. Enjoy!

28: Indian Style Apricot Chicken

Serves: 4 people   **Prep Time:** 20 mins   **Cooking Time:** 11 mins   **Smart Points:** 8

Ingredients:

1. 2 1/2 pounds' of chicken thighs, skinless
2. 1/2 teaspoon of salt
3. 1/4 teaspoon of black pepper
4. 1 teaspoon of vegetable oil
5. 1 large onion, chopped
6. 1/2 cup of chicken broth
7. 1 tablespoon of ginger, freshly grated
8. 2 cloves of garlic, minced
9. 1/2 teaspoon of ground cinnamon
10. 1/8 teaspoon of ground allspice
11. 1 can diced tomatoes
12. 1 package of dried apricots
13. 1 pinch of saffron threads, optional
14. Italian parsley, optional

Directions:

1. Season the chicken with salt and pepper, then cook the chicken in batches using the 'Sauté' mode of the Instant Pot for 8 minutes on each batch. Remove the chicken and place it in a plate.
2. Add the onion and 2 tablespoons of chicken broth to the pot, then cook for 5 minutes until the onion is translucent, while making sure to scrap the burnt ones from the bottom of the pot.
3. Add the ginger, garlic, cinnamon, allspice and cook for 30 seconds until it starts producing fragrance. Pour in the tomatoes, apricots, the remaining broth, saffron, and mix properly. Return the chicken to the Instant Pot, and cook on high pressure for 11 minutes using the 'Manual' setting.
4. Once done, use a quick release to get rid of the pressure, season it with salt and pepper, then garnish it with parsley if desired. Enjoy!

29: Honey Garlic Chicken Lettuce Wraps

Serves: 4 to 6 people

Prep Time: 30 minutes   **Cooking Time:** 30 minutes   **Smart Points:** 8

Ingredients:

1. 2 tablespoons of coconut aminos
2. 1/8 cup of honey garlic sauce
3. 1/4 teaspoon of chilies
4. 1 tablespoon of onion, minced
5. 1/2 teaspoon of salt
6. 1 teaspoon of black pepper
7. 8 to 10 chicken thighs, bone and skinless
8. 1 jalapeno, sliced(optional)
9. 1 head lettuce
10. 1 medium carrot, finely grated
11. 1/2 bell of pepper, thinly sliced
12. 1 green onion, diced
13. 1 avocado, thinly sliced
14. 1/8 cup of cashews, chopped

Directions:

1. Combine the coconut aminos, onions, chilies, salt, pepper and the honey garlic sauce in a bowl. Add the chicken to the mixture and let it soak for 20 to 40 minutes.
2. Put the chicken , the sauce, in the Instant Pot, and cook on a high pressure for 6 minutes using the 'Manual' mode. While waiting for that, you can chop, grate the ingredients listed above and prepare the lettuce into full leaves.
3. Once the time is exhausted, let the pressure manually release. Thereafter, leave it in the sauce until you are ready to wrap it up. Then place the chicken, carrot, pepper, cashews, onions and avocado in the leaves of the lettuce, and roll it up. Serve and enjoy!

30: Teriyaki Chicken and Rice

Serves: 4 to 6 people

Prep Time: 25 minutes

Cooking Time: 30 minutes

Smart Points: 8

Ingredients:

1. 6 chicken thighs, bone-in with skin
2. 1 slice of ginger, very thin
3. 4 crushed garlic cloves
4. 1 1/2 tablespoons of cornstarch, mixed with 2 tablespoons of water
5. teriyaki sauce
6. 4 tablespoons of Japanese Cooking Rice Wine
7. 4 tablespoons of Japanese soy sauce
8. 4 tablespoons of Japanese cooking sake
9. 1/4 teaspoon of sesame oil
10. 2 tablespoons of white sugar
11. 1 1/2 cup of water
12. 1 cup of calrose rice, medium grain

Directions:

1. Mix the soy sauce, sake, mirin, sugar and sesame oil to create the teriyaki sauce mixture. Then soak the chicken with the sauce for 20 minutes.
2. Pour the marinade (without the chicken) into the Instant Pot and cook using the 'Sauté' mode. Add the garlic cloves, ginger, to the mixture and let it boil for 30 seconds or until the alcohol evaporates.
3. Add the chicken to the Instant Pot, pour the rice into a steamer rack, insert it into the pressure cooker and pour the water into the bowl of rice, making sure all of it is soaked in the water.

4. Cover the lid and cook on a high pressure for 6 minutes. When the time is up, use the quick pressure release to remove the pressure.
5. Set the rice, chicken, ginger and garlic aside, and heat the remaining seasoning using the 'Sauté' mode. Add the cornstarch into the sauce slowly until you reach your desired thickness. Then serve immediately with rice and other side dishes. Enjoy!

31: Salt Baked Chicken

Serves: 8 people

Prep Time: 5 minutes

Cooking Time: 45 minutes

Smart Points: 7

Ingredients:

1. 2 teaspoons of sand ginger, dried
2. 1 1/4 teaspoon of kosher salt
3. 1/4 teaspoon of 5 spice powder
4. 8 chicken drumsticks

Directions:

1. Season the chicken legs by covering it with a mixture of kosher salt, 5 spice powder and a sand ginger. Mix properly and place the seasoned legs on a large piece of parchment paper (Do not use aluminum foil).
2. Place the steamer rack above the Instant Pot and pour one cup of water on it. Place the legs dish into the rack and cover the lid of the pot. Cook on a high pressure for 20 minutes, and then let the pressure release naturally.
3. Remove the dish from the Instant Pot and carefully unwrap the parchment paper. Serve immediately. Enjoy!

32: Chinese Simmered Chicken

Serves: 6 people   **Prep Time:** 6 mins   **Cooking Time:** 15 mins   **Smart Points:** 7

Ingredients:

1. 1/3 cup of soy sauce
2. 1/3 cup of brown sugar
3. 1/4 cup of water
4. 1/4 cup of dry sherry or apple juice
5. 1 tablespoon of ketchup
6. 1/2 teaspoon of red pepper flakes, crushed
7. 1 clove garlic, minced
8. 1 scallion sliced
9. 2 tablespoons of cornstarch
10. 2 teaspoons of sesame seeds
11. rice, cooked
12. 4 pounds' of chicken, boneless and skinless
13. 1 tablespoon of olive oil

Directions:

1. Combine the soy sauce, sugar, water, sherry, ketchup, red pepper flakes, garlic, and scallion into a mixing bowl and whisk properly. This will be your sauce.
2. Select the 'Sauté' mode on the Instant Pot and pour the oil into the pot. Lightly sear the chicken in the pot and deglaze the Instant Pot with the sherry and add the sauce, while mixing properly.
3. Add the rice, and cover the lid. Cook at a high pressure for 6 minutes, and when the time is up, use a natural pressure release, and select the 'Sauté' mode again.
4. Remove the rice, chicken, the half cup of the sauce into a platter and add the potato starch into the remaining sauce in the Instant Pot. Cook until the sauce is thick and sticky.
5. Pour the thickened sauce over the chicken, serve with rice and theremaining sauce. Thereafter, garnish it with sesame seeds. Enjoy!

33: Buffalo Hot Wings

Serves: 6 people

Prep Time: 5 minutes

Cooking Time: 15 minutes

Smart Points: 8

Ingredients:

1. 4 pounds' chicken wings
2. 1/2 cup of butter
3. 1/2 cup of Frank's Red Hot Cayenne Pepper Sauce
4. 1 tablespoon of Worcestershire sauce
5. 1/2 teaspoon of kosher salt
6. 3/4 cup of water
7. 1 to 2 tablespoon of light brown sugar

Directions:

1. Mix the pepper sauce, butter, Worcestershire, brown sugar , salt, and microwave all of it for 15 seconds, or until the butter is melted.
2. Pour the water into the Instant Pot, and place the wings on a trivet. Cook at a high pressure for 5 minutes with the lid covered. When done, let the pressure release itself naturally.
3. Place an oven rack in the center of the oven and turn it on to Broil. Brush the chicken wings gently and place them on the oven rack on a cookie sheet. Broil for 5 minutes on each side, or repeat until it gets crispy.
4. Remove the chicken and serve immediately with the remaining sauce. Enjoy!

34: Ligurian Lemon Chicken

Serves: 6 people   **Prep Time:** 10 mins   **Cooking Time:** 15 mins   **Smart Points:** 8

Ingredients:

1. 1 chicken, cut into 8 pieces
2. 1 cup of vegetable or chicken stock
3. 4 ounces' of black olives
4. 1/2 cup of dry white wine
5. 4 lemons, 3 juiced and one for garnish
6. 2 cloves of garlic
7. 3 sprigs of rosemary, one for garnish, and two for chopping
8. 2 sprigs sage
9. 1/2 bunch of Parsley leaves
10. salt and pepper, to taste
11. 4 tablespoons of olive oil

Directions:

1. Prepare the marinade by finely chopping the garlic, sage, parsley and the rosemary. Place them into a container and add the lemon juice, oil, salt, pepper. and mix properly.
2. Place the chicken in a dish and cover it properly with the marinade, a plastic wrap and leave it in the fridge for 4 hours. Using the 'Sauté' mode, cook the chicken for 5 minutes on each sid and when its done , set it aside.
3. Deglaze the Instant Pot with the wine until it evaporates. Add the chicken back in, pour the leftover marinade and place it on top of everything. Thereafter, cover the lid and cook on a high pressure for 12 minutes using the 'Manual' setting.
4. Take the chicken out and reduce the liquid in the pot to about 1/4 of its original amount. Pour the sauce over the chicken, serve with a sprinkle of rosemary, olives and the fresh lemon slices. Enjoy!

35: Not Yo Mama's Chicken Korma

Serves: 6 people

Prep Time: 5 minutes   **Cooking Time:** 20 minutes

Smart Points: 7

Ingredients:

1. 1-pound of chicken, breasts or legs, boneless
2. 1 ounce of cashews, raw
3. 1 small onion, chopped
4. 1/2 cup of tomatoes, diced
5. 1/2 green of Serrano pepper, Thai Chile pepper
6. 5 cloves of garlic
7. 1 teaspoon of Ginger, minced
8. 1 teaspoon of turmeric
9. 1 teaspoon of salt
10. 1 teaspoon of garam masala
11. 1 teaspoon of cumin-coriander powder
12. 1/2 teaspoon of cayenne pepper
13. 1/2 cup of water, for sloshing the blender and for preheating the Instant Pot
14. 1 teaspoon of garam masala, for finishing
15. 1/2 cup of coconut milk, full fat
16. 1/4 cup of cilantro

Directions:

1. Blend all the ingredients except for the chicken, garam masala, coconut milk and cilantro. Pour the sauce in the Instant Pot, top it with the chicken and cook on a high pressure for 10 minutes.
2. When the time is up, let the pressure release naturally. After that, take the chicken out and cut it into small pieces. Then add the coconut milk and garam masala, garnish it with the cilantro and serve. Enjoy!

36: Salsa Chicken

Serves: 4 to 5 people

Prep Time: 5 minutes

Cooking Time: 25 minutes

Smart Points: 8

Ingredients:

1. 2 chicken breasts, boneless and skinless
2. sea salt
3. Mexican seasoning (chili, taco or fajita)
4. 1 cup of salsa, your preference

Direction:

1. Season the chicken with salt and other seasonings on both sides. Place the breasts directly in the Instant Pot, and top it with the salsa. Cook for 10 minutes on a high pressure using the 'Manual' mode.
2. Then when time is exhausted, let the pressure release naturally for 10 minutes. Use the tongs to transfer the chicken and the forks to shred the chicken into small pieces.
3. Serve it with the casseroles, or simply add to the corn tortillas, some avocado, cilantro and lime juice for a quick meal. Enjoy!

37: Turkey and White Bean Chili

Serves: 4 people

Prep Time: 10 minutes   **Cooking Time:** 50 minutes

Smart Points: 8

Ingredients:

1. 1 tablespoon of olive oil
2. 1/2 cup of Anahiem pepper, diced
3. 2 cups of yellow onion, diced
4. 1-pound of ground turkey
5. 1/2 cup of red bell pepper, diced
6. 1 tablespoon of salt
7. 1/2 teaspoon of black pepper
8. 1 teaspoon of oregano
9. 2 tablespoons of chili powder
10. 1 cup of cannellini beans, pre-soaked for 12 hours
11. 2 1/2 cups of chicken stock
12. sour cream, for serving
13. cilantro, chopped for serving
14. Spicy Monterey Jack cheese, for serving

Directions:

1. Set Instant Pot to the 'Sauté' mode and add the oil, onion and peppers. Cook it the onions become brownish.. Then add the turkey, seasonings, and heat it until it gets almost cooked, about 10 minutes.
2. Add the beans, water and the chicken stock. Cover the lid and cook it for 30 minutes using the 'Bean/Chili' mode. When the time is up, release the pressure and serve it with the sour cream, cilantro and Spicy Monterey Jack cheese. Enjoy!

38: Mergherita Chicken with Sundried Tomato Sauce

Serves: 4 people

Prep Time: 10 minutes   **Cooking Time:** 25 minutes   **Smart Points:** 7

Ingredients:

1. 1/4 cup of balsamic vinegar
2. 1 tablespoon of olive oil
3. 2 tablespoons of Dijon mustard
4. 2 tablespoons of lemon juice
5. 2 cloves of garlic, minced
6. 1/2 teaspoon of Himalayan salt
7. 1/4 teaspoon of pepper
8. 6 chicken breasts, boneless and skinless
9. 2 teaspoons of butter
10. 1 cup of chicken bone broth
11. 1/2 cup of sundried tomatoes
12. 1 tablespoon of parsley
13. 1 teaspoon of lemon zest

Directions:

1. Whisk the mustard, vinegar, lemon juice, olive oil, pepper and the garlic salt in small bowl. Mix the vinaigrette, chicken pieces, in a plastic bag and cover by tossing it.
2. Refrigerate it for at least 2 hours to one day. Set the Instant Pot to the 'sauté' mode, melt the butter and get the chicken breasts brown.
3. Remove the chicken from the cooker and deglaze the Pot with chicken bone broth. Add the sundried tomatoes, parsley, lemon zest and return the chicken to the Instant Pot.
4. Cook on a high pressure for 8 minutes on the 'Manual' mode, and when the time is up, allow the pressure to release. Serve and Enjoy!

39: Lemon and Herb Chicken

Serves: 6 people

Prep Time: 20 minutes

Cooking Time: 25 minutes

Smart Points: 8

Ingredients:

1. 4 pounds of white chicken
2. 1 tablespoon of olive oil
3. 1 tablespoon of butter, melted
4. 1/2 teaspoon of black pepper
5. 1 teaspoon of Pink Himalayan salt
6. 1 cup of chicken bone broth
7. 1/2 yellow onion, quartered
8. 1/2 lemon, sliced
9. several sprig of herbs
10. 1 cup of chicken bone broth

Directions:

1. Rub the chicken breast with the olive oil, butter and season it with the salt and pepper. Preheat the Instant Pot using the 'Sauté' mode, and place the chicken in the Pot.
2. Brown the chicken for at least 2 minutes or until the chicken turns a fully golden brown color. Remove the chicken to a place and deglaze the pan with the bone broth.
3. Put the lemons, garlic, onion and fresh herbs into the cavity of the whole chicken and return it to the Instant Pot. Using the 'Manual' mode, cook the chicken for 20 minutes on a high pressure.
4. Transfer the chicken to the plate, and serve with the broth. Enjoy!

40: Honey Garlic Chicken Wings

Serves: 4 people

Prep Time: 10 minutes

Cooking Time: 10 minutes

Smart Points: 8

Ingredients:

1. 1 1/2 pounds' of chicken wings
2. 1/2 shallot, roughly minced
3. 1 to 2-star anise
4. 1 tablespoon of ginger, sliced
5. 4 cloves of garlic, roughly minced
6. 1 tablespoon of honey
7. 1/2 cup of water, warm
8. 1 1/2 tablespoon of cornstarch
9. 1 tablespoon of peanut oil
10. 2 tablespoon of light soy sauce
11. 1 tablespoon of dark soy sauce
12. 1 teaspoon of sugar
13. 1 tablespoon of Shaoxing wine
14. 1/4 teaspoon of salt

Directions:

1. Make the marinade by mixing the light and dark soy sauce, Shaoxing wine, sugar and the salt. Soak the chicken wings for 20 minutes.
2. Heat up the Instant Pot using the 'Sauté' mode and add the peanut oil to the base. Add the chicken wings, then brown the chicken wings for 30 seconds on each side. Then remove and set it aside.
3. Add the shallot, star anise, sliced ginger and then stir for a minute. Add the garlic and continue stirring until it produces some fragrance. Mix the honey with a warm water and add it to the bottom of the pot. Place the chicken wings into

the pot, cover the lid and cook it on a high pressure for 5 minutes using the 'Manual' mode.

4. Once the time is up, remove the chicken wings only. Using the sauté mode, add the cornstarch with one tablespoon of cold water and then keep mixing until it gets to your desired thickness.

5. Add the chicken wings back into the Instant Pot and then transfer all of it to a large bowl. Serve immediately. Enjoy!

Vegetarian

41: Cauliflower Potato Curry

Serves: 4 people

Prep Time: 10 minutes   **Cooking Time:** 10 minutes   **Smart Points:** 5

Ingredients:

1. 1 medium sized onion, thinly sliced
2. 2 plum tomatoes, diced
3. 1 medium potato, cut into wedges
4. 4 cups of cauliflower, big 2 inch pieces
5. 1 tablespoon of cooking oil
6. 1/2 teaspoon of cumin
7. 1/2 teaspoon of turmeric
8. 1 teaspoon of mild red chili powder
9. 1 tablespoon of cumin-coriander
10. 1 teaspoon of salt
11. 1 1/2 teaspoon of garam masala

Directions:

1. Preheat the Instant Pot using the 'Sauté' mode. Add the oil, cumin and sauté it for 30 seconds. Add the onions and cook it for an additional 1 minute. Add the tomatoes and cook for 1 more minute too.
2. Add the turmeric, red chili powder, cumin-coriander, garam masala, the salt and keep mixing properly. Add the potatoes, cauliflower and 1/4 cup of water as well.
3. Cover the lid and cook for 3 minutes on high pressure using the 'Manual' mode. Increase the time by 2 minutes if you want a firmer cauliflower.
4. When the time is up, quick release the pressure and take the curry out of the Instant Pot. Serve it with a toasted pita bread. Enjoy!

42: BBQ Cabbage Sandwiches

Serves: 6 people

Prep Time: 5 minutes

Cooking Time: 10 minutes

Smart Points: 3

Ingredients:

1. 1 head cabbage, chopped
2. 1 yellow onion, small and thinly sliced
3. 2 1/2 cups of BBQ sauce
4. 6 buns, whole wheat and gluten free

Directions:

1. Preheat the Instant Pot using the 'Sauté' mode, and add 2 tablespoons of water to the pot. Add cabbage, onion, and heat it until they are softened, usually at about 4 minutes. Thereafter, add the BBQ sauce and cook for 3 more minutes.
2. Stop the 'Sauté' mode, toast the buns, fill them with thee BBQ cabbage and serve immediately. Enjoy!

43: BBQ Lentils over Baked Potato Wedges

Serves: 4 people

Prep Time: 5 minutes

Cooking Time: 20 minutes

Smart Points: 3

Ingredients:

1. 3 cup of water
2. 1 small onion, chopped
3. 1/2 cup of ketchup, organic
4. 1 cup of brown lentils, dry and drained
5. 2 teaspoons of liquid smoke
6. 2 teaspoons of molasses
7. 2 large potatoes, baked and cut into 6 wedges

Directions:

1. Place the lentils, water, the onion in the Instant Pot and cook for 10 minutes on a high pressure using the 'Manual' mode. When the time is up, let the pressure naturally release.
2. Add the ketchup, molasses, liquid smoke to the pot and then using the 'Sauté' mode, simmer it for 5 minutes. When the time is up, stop the 'Sauté' mode and serve it over some baked potato wedges. Enjoy!

44: Bell Peppers and Stir Fried Potatoes

Serves: 2 people

Prep Time: 5 minutes

Cooking Time: 15 minutes

Smart Points: 4

Ingredients:

1. 1 tablespoon of oil
2. 2 bell pepper, cut into long pieces
3. 1/2 teaspoon of cumin seeds
4. 4 baby potatoes, cut into small pieces
5. 1/2 teaspoon of dry mango
6. 1/4 teaspoon of turmeric
7. 1/2 teaspoon of cayenne
8. 2 teaspoon of coriander
9. 1 teaspoon of salt
10. 4 cloves of garlic
11. cilantro, for garnishing

Directions:

1. Preheat the Instant Pot using the 'Sauté' mode, add the oil, cumin and garlic. Once the garlic turns golden brown, add the peppers, spices and potatoes. Thereafter, sprinkle the water and mix properly.
2. Change the mode to 'Manual' and cook on a high pressure for 2 minutes. When done, release the pressure manually. If the mixture is watery, simmer it using the 'Sauté' mode with the lid open and stir until you get the desired consistency.
3. Add the dry mango or lemon juice and mix evenly. Garnish it with the cilantro and serve with a yogurt. Enjoy!

45: Black Bean Mushroom Chili

Serves: 4 to 6 people

Prep Time: 5 minutes   **Cooking Time:** 16 minutes   **Smart Points:** 4

Ingredients:

1. 3 cups of onion, chopped
2. 8 cloves of garlic, finely minced
3. 2 pounds' of mushrooms, sliced
4. 2 cans of fire roasted tomatoes
5. 16 ounces' of corn, frozen
6. 3 cans of black beans, including liquid
7. 1 tablespoon of grounded cumin
8. 1 oregano
9. 1/2 tablespoon of smoked paprika
10. 1/2 teaspoon of ground chipotle powder
11. 1 cup of oats
12. 1 cup of nutritional yeast
13. 1 tablespoon of salt-free seasoning

Directions:

1. Preheat the Instant Pot using the 'Sauté' mode, then heat the onions until they are brown at about 10 minutes, while constantly adding small amounts of water to prevent sticking. Then add the garlic and heat it for one more minute.
2. Change the mode to 'Manual' and add all the ingredients except for the corn and the Faux Parmesan. Cook on a high pressure for 6 minutes, and let the pressure naturally release.
3. While the dish is cooking, place the faux ingredients into a food processor and grind until it turns into powder. This powder is usually known as the Faux Parmesan.
4. When the pressure is released, pour the curry into a bowl. Stir in the corn and sprinkle the Faux Parmesan on topof it. Enjoy!

46: Chickpea Curry

Serves: 4 to 6 people

Prep Time: 10 minutes   **Cooking Time:** 5 minutes   **Smart Points:** 5

Ingredients:

1. 1 onion, diced
2. 2 cloves of garlic, minced
3. 2 tablespoons of extra-virgin olive oil
4. 1 small green bell pepper, diced
5. 2 cans of chickpeas, rinsed and drained
6. 1 can of tomatoes, crushed or diced, with juice
7. 1 tablespoon of curry powder
8. 1 cup of corn, frozen
9. 1 packed cup of kale, chopped
10. 1 cup of okra, frozen and sliced
11. 1 cup of vegetable broth
12. 1 tablespoon of honey or sugar
13. 1 teaspoon of kosher salt
14. 1/4 teaspoon of black pepper, freshly grounded
15. 2 tablespoon of cilantro leaves, for garnishing
16. 1 lime, juiced.

Directions:

1. Preheat the Instant Pot using the 'Sauté' mode, add the oil and onion. Cook for 4 minutes, then add the bell pepper, garlic and cook for 2 more minutes.
2. Add the curry powder and stir it for 30 seconds. Add the chickpeas, tomatoes, corn, okra, kale, broth, and honey (or sugar). Cover the lid and cook for 5 minutes on a high pressure using the 'Manual' mode. Once the cooking is done, let the pressure naturally release.
3. Add the salt, pepper, and lime juice. Stir it until it mixes properly, while adding more salt as desired. Top it with the cilantro leaves and serve. Enjoy!

47: Couscous and Vegetable Medley

Serves: 3 people

Prep Time: 5 minutes

Cooking Time: 20 minutes

Smart Points: 4

Ingredients:

1. 1 tablespoon of olive oil
2. 2 bay leaves, or Taj Patta
3. 1 large red bell pepper, chopped
4. 1/2 large onion, chopped
5. 1 3/4 cup of couscous Israeli
6. 1 cup of carrot, grated
7. 1 3/4 cup of water
8. 2 teaspoon of salt, according to taste
9. 1/2 teaspoon of garam masala
10. 1 tablespoon of lemon juice
11. cilantro, for garnishing

Directions:

1. Preheat the Instant Pot to the 'sauté' mode and add the olive oil, bay leaves and onions. Heat it for 2 minutes, add the bell peppers, carrots and sauté it for one more minute. Add the couscous, water, salt, garam masala and mix properly.
2. Change the mode to 'Manual' and cook for 2 minutes. When the time is up, do a 10-minute natural pressure release and fluff the couscous until it is fully cooked. Mix the lemon juice, garnish it with the cilantro and serve it hot. Enjoy!

48: Kashmiri Potato Curry

Serves: 3 people   **Prep Time:** 10 mins   **Cooking Time:** 20 mins   **Smart Points:** 3

Ingredients:

1. 10 baby potatoes, peeled and cored.
2. 1 onion, finely chopped
3. 2 tablespoons of ghee
4. 2 teaspoons of ginger, grated
5. 2 red tomatoes, pureed
6. 2 teaspoon of garlic, grated
7. 1/2 teaspoon of turmeric
8. 1 teaspoon of Kashmiri red chili powder
9. 1 teaspoon of salt
10. 8 to 10 cashews
11. 1/4 cup of warm milk
12. 1 tablespoon of dried fenugreek leaves
13. some cilantro leaves

Directions:

1. Preheat the Instant Pot using the 'Sauté' mode. Add the ghee, onions and cook for 2 minutes while constantly stirring, then add the ginger, potatoes and garlic paste for 30 seconds.
2. Add the tomato paste, red chili powder, turmeric, garam masala and salt. Cook everything for two minutes while constantly stirring. With a small spoon, carefully fill the potatoes and line them all in the space of the Instant Pot.
3. Add 1.2 cup of water, cover the lid, then cook for 8 minutes on a high pressure using the 'Manual' mode. When the time is up, quickly release the pressure.
4. Blend the milk and cashews to make a smooth paste, then add the liquid, dried fenugreek leaves, cashew paste and the cilantro leaves. Set the nstant Pot to the 'Sauté' mode and mix together. Add the salt, then turn the Instant Pot off.
5. Serve with rice. Enjoy!

49: Easy Potato Beans

Serves: 3 people

Prep Time: 5 minutes   **Cooking Time:** 10 minutes   **Smart Points:** 4

Ingredients:

1. 1 tablespoon of oil
2. 4 cloves of garlic, chopped
3. 1/2 teaspoon of cumin seeds
4. 1 green chili, chopped
5. 2 cup of green beans, 1/2 inch pieces
6. 1 potato, cubed into small pieces
7. 2 teaspoons of coriander powder
8. 1/4 teaspoon of turmeric
9. 1/4 teaspoon of red chili
10. 1 1/2 teaspoons of salt
11. 1 teaspoon of dry mango,

Directions:

1. Preheat the Instant Pot using the 'Sauté' mode. Add the oil, cumin seeds, green chili and garlic. When the seeds start to splutter, add the green beans and potatoes. Combine all the spices except the dry mango, and mix properly. Thereafter, sprinkle some water on top of it.
2. Secure the Instant Pot, and cook for 2 minutes on a high pressure using the 'Manual' mode. When the time is up, let the pressure naturally release itself. Mix the dry mango into the curry,serve with a bread and enjoy!

50: Green Coconut Curry

Serves: 4 people

Prep Time: 5 minutes   **Cooking Time:** 15 minutes   **Smart Points:** 4

Ingredients:

1. 1/2 cup of chickpeas, soaked for 6 hours
2. 1 small onion, diced
3. 2 cloves of garlic, minced
4. 1 teaspoon of turmeric, freshly minced
5. 2 teaspoons of ginger, freshly minced
6. 1 can of coconut milk
7. 1/2 cup of vegetable stock
8. 1 tablespoon of green curry paste
9. 1/2 teaspoon of cumin
10. 1/2 teaspoon of black pepper
11. 1 teaspoon of salt
12. 1/2 teaspoon of curry
13. 1/4 teaspoon of ground coriander
14. 1/4 teaspoon of chili powder
15. 1 cup of spinach
16. 2 teaspoon of lemon juice

Directions:

1. Preheat the Instant Pot using the 'Sauté' mode and add the onions. Heat it until they are brownish, then add the ginger, garlic and turmeric. Sauté it for 2 more minutes and add all the remaining ingredients except for the lemon juice and spinach.
2. Cover the lid and change the mode to 'Manual'. Cook on a high pressure for 15 minutes and when the time has elapsed, allow a natural pressure release.
3. Add the spinach and lemon juice on top and stir well. Serve and Enjoy!

51: Instant Potatouille

Serves: 4 people

Prep Time: 5 minutes

Cooking Time: 10 minutes

Smart Points: 4

Ingredients:

1. 1/4 cup of water
2. 4 ounces of Yellow Crookneck Squash
3. 4 ounces of Zucchini
4. 6 ounces of Chinese Eggplant
5. 4 ounces of Orange Bell Pepper
6. 3 ounces of Portobello mushrooms
7. 1/4 red onion
8. 12 ounces of Yukon gold potatoes, about 1 1/2 pounds
9. 1 can of Fire Roasted Tomatoes
10. 1/4 cup of basil, finely chopped into threads

Directions:

1. Put all the ingredients except the basil into into the Instant Pot and cook on a high pressure for 10 minutes using the 'Manual' mode. Once done, quick release the pressure and pour in the basil.
2. Serve it with rice if desired. Enjoy!

52: Italian Cannellini and Mint Salad

Serves: 4 people

Prep Time: 1 minute

Cooking Time: 8 minutes

Smart Points: 5

Ingredients:

1. 1 cup of cannellini beans, soaked in water
2. 4 cups of warm water
3. 1 clove of garlic, smashed
4. 1 bay leaf
5. 1 sprig mint, fresh
6. 1 dash of vinegar
7. olive oil
8. salt and pepper, to taste

Directions:

1. Place the beans, water, garlic and bay leaf into the Instant Pot, cover the lid and cook on a high pressure for 8 minutes using the 'Manual' mode. When the time has elapsed, use a natural pressure release.
2. Mix the mint, vinegar, oil, salt, pepper and stir well. Serve and Enjoy!

53: Lemon-Sage Spaghetti Squash

Serves: 4 people

Prep Time: 15 minutes   **Cooking Time:** 9 minutes

Smart Points: 5

Ingredients:

1. 2 pounds' of spaghetti squash, cut into half
2. 1 cup of water
3. 2 tablespoons of butter
4. 1/4 cup of onion, chopped
5. 2 garlic cloves, minced
6. 2 tablespoons of Parmesan cheese, grated
7. 2 tablespoons of sage leaves, finely chopped
8. 1 teaspoon of lemon rind, grated
9. 1/2 teaspoon of table salt
10. 1/4 teaspoon of black pepper, grounded

Directions:

1. Place a steam rack in the inner pot of the Instant Pot, and pour the water. Add the squash halves, and cook at a high pressure for 9 minutes using the 'Manual' mode. When done, lift the squash using rack handles and set it aside to cool down.
2. While the squash is cooling, pour the water the from the inner pot,rinse it well,dry it and return it to the cooker. When the squash cools down, use a fork to remove the spaghetti-like strands in a bowl.
3. Add the butter into the Instant Pot, and heat it using the 'Sauté' mode. When the butter melts, add the onion,garlic and cook for 2 minutes while constantly stirring. Then, add the squash to the pot, stir for 2 more minutes and transfer again to the bowl.
4. Add the Parmesan cheese and other ingredients on top and serve. Enjoy!

54: Lentil and Red Bean Chili

Serves: 6 people   **Prep Time:** 15 mins   **Cooking Time:** 45 mins   **Smart Points:** 5

Ingredients:

1. 1/2 cup of brown and red lentils, soaked in water overnight
2. 1/2 cup of yellow onion, chopped
3. 1 cup of carrot, chopped
4. 1 green bell pepper, chopped
5. 5 cloves of garlic, minced
6. 1 teaspoon of smoked paprika
7. 1 1/2 teaspoons of chili powder
8. 1/2 teaspoon of coriander powder
9. 1 teaspoon of cumin powder
10. 1/2 teaspoon of dried oregano
11. 1/2 teaspoon of allspice
12. 1/2 teaspoon of cayenne powder
13. 1 teaspoon of salt
14. 2 tablespoons of coconut aminos
15. 1 can of tomatoes, diced
16. 1/4 heaping cup of tomato paste
17. 1 1/2 cups of water
18. 1 cup of corn

Directions:

1. Preheat the Instant Pot using the 'Sauté' mode, add the carrots, onions, garlic, bell pepper and sauté for 3 to 5 minutes, stirring occasionally.
2. Add all the spices, salt, coconut aminos, tomatoes, tomato paste and beans. Stir for one minute then add the water and stir once more.
3. Cover the lid of the Instant Pot and cook for 30 minutes on a high pressure using the 'Manual' mode. Once done, let the pressure naturally release. Then after opening the lid, add the corn and stir properly.
4. Allow the chili to cool off before you serve or store in the fridge. Enjoy!

55: Lentils and Farro

Serves: 2 people

Prep Time: 2 minutes

Cooking Time: 12 minutes

Smart Points: 4

Ingredients:

1. 1/2 cup of lentils, brown, black or green
2. 1 1/4 cup of water
3. 1/2 teaspoon of medium chili powder
4. 1/2 teaspoon of dried oregano
5. 1/2 teaspoon of salt
6. 1/2 teaspoon of dried basil
7. 1/4 teaspoon of cumin powder
8. 1/4 teaspoon of smoked paprika
9. 1/4 teaspoon of onion powder
10. 1/4 teaspoon of garlic powder
11. 1/4 teaspoon of black pepper
12. 1/2 cup of Farro, for Farro
13. 1 cup of water, for Farro
14. 1/2 teaspoon of Italian herbs, for Farro
15. 1/2 teaspoon of onion powder, for Farro
16. 1/2 teaspoon of salt, for Farro

Directions:

1. Add all the ingredients except the Farro ones into the Instant Pot. Place the trivet on top of lentils, add the faro ingredients in it and cover the lid. Cook for 12 minutes on a high pressure using the 'Manual' mode.
2. When the time has elapsed, let the pressure naturally release. Serve it with your favorite veggies and sauces. Enjoy!

56: Middle Eastern Millet Pilaf

Serves: 4 people

Prep Time: 5 minutes

Cooking Time: 10 minutes

Smart Points: 4

Ingredients:

1. 1 tablespoon of oil
2. 1 cup of onion, chopped
3. 2 cloves of garlic, minced
4. 1 stick of cinnamon
5. 1 cup of carrots, roughly chopped
6. 1 cup of millet
7. 1 3/4 cups of water
8. salt, to taste
9. pepper, to taste
10. Italian parsley, chopped

Directions:

1. Heat the oil in the Instant Pot using the 'Sauté' mode. Add the onions and heat it for one minute. Add the garlic, carrots, cinnamon stick and heat it for 30 more seconds. Thereafter, add the millet, water and stir.
2. Cover the lid of the Instant Pot and cook for 10 minutes on a high pressure using the 'Manual' mode. Once done, let the pressure naturally release. Then remove the cinnamon stick.
3. Fluff the salt, parsley, pepper on top of it and mix well. Enjoy!

57: Mixed Vegetable and Lentil Curry

Serves: 6 people   **Prep Time:** 10 mins   **Cooking Time:** 30 mins   **Smart Points:** 3

Ingredients:

1. 2 tablespoons of ghee
2. 1 teaspoon of cumin seeds
3. 1 tablespoon of Ginger
4. 1 carrot, peeled and sliced
5. 1/4 cup of green peas, frozen
6. 1/4 cup of green beans, chopped
7. 1 red potato, cubed
8. 1 tomato, diced
9. 1 cup of cabbage, chopped
10. 1 cup of cauliflower, chopped
11. 1 cup of spinach, chopped
12. 1/2 teaspoon of turmeric
13. 2 teaspoons of red chili powder
14. 2 teaspoon of salt
15. 1 cup of white rice
16. 1 cup of mixed lentils
17. 6 cups of water
18. 1/4 cup of cilantro, chopped for garnishing

Directions:

1. Preheat the Instant Pot using the 'Sauté' mode and add the ghee, cumin seeds and ginger. Cook it for 30 seconds, then add all the vegetables and mix properly. Add the turmeric, red chili powder, salt, rice ,the mixed lentils and stir properly.
2. Add 6 cups of water. Give everything a quick stir, and once done, cover the lid of the Instant Pot. Cook it for 12 minutes using the 'Rice' mode, and when the time is up, let the pressure naturally release.
3. Open the Instant Pot and transfer the curry to a large bowl. Garnish it with the cilantro and serve it hot with bread and pickles. Enjoy!

58: Not Re-Fried Beans

Serves: 6 to 8 people

Prep Time: 5 minutes   **Cooking Time:** 10 minutes   **Smart Points:** 5

Ingredients:

1. 1 tablespoon of oil
2. 1 onion, chopped
3. 1 bunch of cilantro, or parsley
4. 1/4 teaspoon of chipotle powder
5. 1/2 teaspoon of cumin
6. 2 cups borlotti of beans, dried
7. 2 cups of water
8. 1 teaspoon of salt

Directions:

1. Preheat the Instant Pot using the 'Sauté' mode. Add the oil, onions, cilantro stems, chipotle, cumin seeds and heat it until the onions begin to get softened.
2. Add the beans, water and cover the lid of the Instant Pot. Cook on a high pressure for 10 minutes using the 'Manual' mode. When the time is up, let the pressure naturally release.
3. Remove a heaping spoon of beans for garnishing, and sprinkle the rest in the cooker with salt. Mash the beans with a potato masher to the desired consistency.
4. Serve it with the sprinkled whole beans, parsley and some optional sour cream. Enjoy!

59: Chinese Steamed Eggs

Serves: 2 people

Prep Time: 5 minutes

Cooking Time: 15 minutes

Smart Points: 7

Ingredients:

1. 2 extra large eggs
2. 1 cup of chicken stock, homemade preferred
3. 1/4 teaspoon of sea salt
4. green onions, for garnishing
5. 1/2 tablespoon of light soy sauce
6. 1/2 tablespoon of fish sauce
7. 1 tablespoon of water

Directions:

1. Beat the eggs until the egg yolks and egg whites have fully been beaten. Then, add the chicken stock, sea salt and mix properly. Pour the mixture into another dish using a strainer, so that it will filter all the lumps produced in the process.
2. Tightly cover the dish with an aluminum foil. Don't forget to follow this step, or else the eggs will become crumble.
3. Place a trivet in the Instant Pot and pour 1 cup of water on it. Carefully place the egg dish into the trivet., cover the lid and cook for 6 minutes on a high pressure using the 'Manual' mode. When the time is up, let the pressure naturally release.
4. While the dish is cooking, make the soy sauce mixture by mixing the soy sauce, fish sauce and one tablespoon of water.
5. Open the lid and carefully remove the aluminum foil. Then garnish the dish with the green onions and pour the soy sauce mix over the eggs. Serve immediately and enjoy!

60: Quick Dry Beans

Serves: 3 people

Prep Time: 1 minutes

Cooking Time: 2 minutes

Smart Points: 6

Ingredients:

1. 1 cup of beans
2. 4 cups of water
3. 1 teaspoon of salt, optional

Directions:

1. Place the water, beans and salt into the Instant Pot. Cook for 2 to 8 minutes at a high pressure using the 'Manual' mode. Once the time is up, let the pressure naturally release.
2. Rinse and drain the beans, if you want to, you can add it to any recipe, or can eat it raw. Note that, if you want fewer amount of beans, you can reduce the ingredients of this recipe as much as you like, but ensure to keep the bean to a water ratio of 1:4. Enjoy!

61: Red Coconut Curry

Serves: 4 people

Prep Time: 5 minutes

Cooking Time: 15 minutes

Smart Points: 5

Ingredients:

1. 1 onion, diced
2. 3/4 cup of chickpeas, soaked overnight
3. 8 ounces' of white mushrooms, sliced
4. 2 garlic cloves, minced
5. 1 small green chili, diced
6. 1/2 tablespoon of turmeric, peeled
7. 1 tablespoon of ginger, peeled
8. 1 can of coconut milk
9. 1/2 cup of vegetable stock
10. 3 tablespoons of red curry paste
11. 1/2 tablespoon of salt
12. 1 teaspoon of cumin
13. 1/2 teaspoon of curry powder
14. 1/4 teaspoon of ground fenugreek
15. 1/4 teaspoon of black pepper
16. 1 tablespoon of tomato paste
17. 1 to 2 teaspoon of lemon juice
18. 1 cup of spinach

Directions:

1. Using the 'Sauté' mode of the Instant Pot, cook the mushrooms until they reduce in size, stirring every couple of minutes. Add the onions, stir and keep cooking until the onions are soft.

2. Add the garlic, chili, ginger, turmeric and heat it for 1 to 2 more minutes. Add all the remaining ingredients (except the tomato paste, lemon juice and spinach) into the Instant Pot and cover the lid.

3. Cook for 15 minutes on a high pressure using the 'Manual' mode. When the time is up, let the pressure naturally release. Then pour in the tomato paste, lemon juice, spinach and serve immediately. Enjoy!

62: Slow Cook Goat Cheese Lasagna

Serves: 8 people

Prep Time: 15 minutes

Cooking Time: 2 hours

Smart Points: 5

Ingredients:

1. 1 tablespoon of oil
2. 1 3/4 cups of onion, chopped
3. 1 cup of zucchini, diced
4. 1/2 cup of carrot, shredded
5. 2 cloves of garlic, chopped
6. 1/2 teaspoon of salt
7. 1/2 teaspoon of black pepper, freshly grounded
8. 1 can of tomatoes, crushed and undrained
9. Cooking spray
10. 1 cup of basil, fresh and chopped
11. 3/4 cup of part-skin ricotta cheese
12. 20 ounces' of spinach, frozen and chopped
13. 2 ounces' of goat cheese, roughly 1/4 cup
14. 8 gluten free lasagna noodles
15. 1-ounce of Parmesan cheese, about 1/4 cup
16. Basil leaves, optional

Directions:

1. Heat a 4-quart saucepan over an average pressure of heat. Add the oil to the pan, and then add the onion, zucchini and carrot. Cook for 5 minutes, then add the garlic, and stir for one more minute. Pour in the salt, pepper , tomatoes and simmer for 5 minutes.
2. Cover the inner pot of the Instant Pot with a cooking spray and mix the basil,

ricotta, spinach and goat cheese in an average sized bowl. Spread 1/2 cup of spinach mix in the cooker, and arrange the noodles over the spinach mixture. Top the half of the remaining spinach mixture and 1 cup the tomato mixture.

3. Cover the lid of the Instant Pot and cook for 2 hours using the 'Slow Cook' mode. When the time is up, let the pressure naturally release. Top the dish with Parmesan cheese and basil leaves. Serve and Enjoy!

63: Smokey Sweet Black Eyed Peas

Serves: 4 people

Prep Time: 5 minutes   **Cooking Time:** 20 minutes   **Smart Points:** 5

Ingredients:

1. 1 tablespoon of oil
2. 1 onion, thinly sliced
3. 2 to 3 cloves of garlic, minced
4. 1 cup of red pepper, diced
5. 1 jalapeno, or any other hot chili
6. 1 to 2 teaspoons of smoked paprika
7. 1 to 2 teaspoons of chili powder
8. 1 1/2 cups of black eyed peas
9. 4 dates, chopped finely
10. 1 cup of water or vegetable broth
11. 1 can of fire roasted tomatoes
12. 2 cups of greens, chopped
13. salt, to taste

Directions:

1. Preheat the Instant Pot using the 'Sauté' mode. Dry heat the onions until they become translucent, adding water if required. Add the garlic, peppers and heat it for another minute. Add the smoked paprika and chili powder along with the peas and dates. Stir to coat them in the spice.
2. Add the water, stirring well to make sure that nothing sticks to the bottom of the pot. Close the lid, and cook at a high pressure for 3 minutes using the 'Manual' mode. Once the time is up and pressure has naturally released, carefully open the lid and add the tomatoes and greens.
3. Thereafter, lock the lid of the Instant Pot for 5 minutes, open it and add the salt to taste. Serve immediately and Enjoy!

Meat & Seafood

64: Spice-rubbed Cauliflower Steaks

Serves: 4 people

Prep Time: 10 minutes

Cooking Time: 5 minutes

Smart Points: 7

Ingredients:

1. 1 large head cauliflower
2. 2 tablespoons of olive oil
3. 2 teaspoons of paprika
4. 2 teaspoons of ground cumin
5. 1 cup of cilantro, fresh and chopped
6. 1 lemon, quartered

Directions:

1. Insert the steam rack into the Instant Pot. Add 1 and a 1/2 cups of water. Remove the leaves from the cauliflower and trim the core so that it sits flat. Thereafter, place it into the steam rack.
2. Using a small bowl, mix the olive oil, paprika, cumin and salt. Drizzle it over the cauliflower and rub it to coat. Cover the lid and cook on a high pressure for 4 minutes using the 'Manual' mode.
3. When the time is up, do a quick pressure release. Lift the cauliflower onto a cutting board and slice it into a 1 inch of steak. Divide it among the plates and sprinkle it with the cilantro. Serve it with the lemon quarters and Enjoy!

65: Herby fish parcel.

Serves: *4.*

Prep time: *5 minutes.*   **Cooking:** *10 minutes on high.*

Smart Points: 7

Ingredients:

4 fillets catfish

2 cups of water

1 diced white onion

3 oz of potatoes, sliced thin

Italian herbs

salt and pepper

olive oil

lemon juice

Directions:

1. Measure your instant pot to ensure your parcel will fit in perfectly.

2. Spread out your parchment paper and alternate the layers of fish, herbs, and vegetables.

3. Tightly wrap it up and put it in a foil.

4. Put the water in the instant pot and drop the fish parcel into the steamer basket.

5. Cook for 10 minutes at a high pressure.

6. Release the pressure naturally and let it rest for 2 minutes, in order to have the juiciest of fishes.

66: Shrimp and Grits

Serves: 4 people

Prep Time: 5 minutes

Cooking Time: 45 minutes

Smart Points: 7

Ingredients:

1. 1-pound of shrimp, deveined
2. 2 teaspoons of old bay seasoning
3. 3 strips if smoked bacon, diced
4. 1/3 cup of onion, chopped finely
5. 1/2 cup of bell peppers, red or green
6. 1 tablespoon of garlic, minced
7. 2 tablespoons of dry white wine
8. 1 1/2 cups of tomatoes, diced
9. 2 tablespoons of lemon juice
10. 1/4 cup of chicken broth
11. 1/4 teaspoon of Tabasco sauce
12. 1/2 teaspoon of salt
13. 1/4 teaspoon of black pepper
14. 1/4 cup of heavy cream
15. 1/4 cup of scallions, thinly sliced
16. 1/2 cup of grits, for grits
17. 1 cup of milk, for grits
18. 1 cup of water, for grits
19. salt, for grits, to taste
20. pepper, for grits, to taste
21. 1 tablespoon of butter, for grits

Directions:

1. Dry the shrimp, sprinkle it with the seasoning and set it aside. Using the 'Sauté' mode, cook the bacon until it gets crisp and brown, at about 4 minutes. Remove it to a plate and set aside.

2. Heat the onions and bell peppers in the bacon fat, at about 2 to 3 minutes. Add the garlic and heat it briefly. Turn the Instant Pot off, deglaze it with the white wine and stir properly to to remove any browned bits.

3. Pour in the tomatoes, lemon juice, broth, hot sauce, salt and pepper. Place the trivet in the Instant Pot. In a medium bowl that fits into the Instant Pot, stir together all the grit ingredients. Place the bowl in the trivet.

4. Close the Instant Pot lid, and cook for 10 minutes on a high pressure using the 'Manual' mode. Once done, allow the pressure to release naturally. Open the Instant Pot, remove the grits and set it aside.

5. Remove the trivet and carefully stir in the shrimp. Close the Pot immediately and let the shrimp cook in the residual heat. After 10 minutes, open the Instant Pot and gently stir the shrimp while adding the cream.

6. Garnish it with the scallions and bacon. Serve the grits topped with shrimp and sauce. Enjoy!

67: Mussels with Red Pepper Garlic Sauce

Serves: 4 people

Prep Time: 15 minutes

Cooking Time: 1 minutes

Smart Points: 9

Ingredients:

1. 1 tablespoon of olive oil
2. 3 pounds of mussels
3. 4 cloves of garlic, minced
4. 1 large red bell pepper, minced
5. 3/4 cup fish stock, clam juice
6. 1/2 cup dry white wine
7. 1/8 teaspoon of red pepper flakes
8. 2 tablespoons of cream, whipping
9. 3 tablespoon of parsley, chopped

Directions:

1. Clean the mussels, preheat the Instant Pot using the 'Sauté' mode, heat the olive oil until it simmers. Thereafter, add the garlic and stir until it produces fragrance. Add the roasted red pepper,, fish stock, wine and the red pepper flakes. Then stir well and combine evenly.
2. Add the mussels to the pot, cover the lid and cook for 1 minute on a high pressure using the 'Manual' mode. When done, do a quick pressure release.
3. Stir in the heavy cream, parsley and serve with cooking liquid. Enjoy!

68: New England Clam Chowder

Serves: 4 to 6 people   **Prep Time:** 5 mins   **Cooking Time:** 10 mins   **Smart Points:** 4

Ingredients:

1. 300 grams' of clams, strained and frozen
2. 2 cups of clam juice
3. 1 cup of bacon, smoked and cured
4. 1 onion, finely chopped
5. 1/2 cup of white wine
6. 2 potatoes, cubed
7. 1 bay leaf
8. 1 sprig thyme
9. 1 pinch of cayenne pepper
10. 1 cup of milk
11. 1 cup of cream
12. 1 teaspoon of butter, melted
13. 1 tablespoon of flour

Directions:

1. Add the cubed bacon to the Instant Pot, and heat it until the bacon begins to sizzle. Add the onion, salt, pepper and raise the heat of the Instant Pot.
2. Once the onions have softened, deglaze using wine and scrape the brown bits on the bottom of the pot. Let the wine evaporate and then add the diced potatoes, clam juice, bay leaf, thyme and the cayenne pepper.
3. Cover the lid and cook for 5 minutes on a high pressure using the 'Manual; mode. While it is cooking, make a roux to thicken the chowder by blending equal amounts of butter and flour over a low heat and stir constantly until they are well blended.
4. When the time is up, do a quick pressure release. Add the roux, milk, cream and clams. Change the mode to the Sauté and simmer all the ingredients for about 5 minutes or so.
5. Serve it with soup crackers or in a fresh bread bowl. Enjoy!

69: Coconut Fish Curry

Serves: 4 people   **Prep Time:** 5 mins   **Cooking Time:** 20 mins   **Smart Points:** 7

Ingredients:

1. 1 1/2 pounds' of white fish fillet
2. 1 heaping cup of cherry tomatoes
3. 2 green chilies, sliced into strips
4. 2 medium onions, sliced into strips
5. 2 cloves of garlic, chopped
6. 1 tablespoon of ginger, freshly grated
7. 6 curry leaves, or bay or basil leaves
8. 1 tablespoon of ground coriander
9. 1 tablespoon of ground cumin
10. 1/2 teaspoon of ground turmeric
11. 1 teaspoon of chili powder
12. 1/2 teaspoon of grounded fenugreek
13. 2 cups of coconut milk, unsweetened
14. salt, to taste
15. lemon juice, to taste

Directions:

1. Using the 'Sauté' mode in the Instant Pot, add the oil and curry leaves. Lightly fry it until they are golden around the edges, at about 1 minute. Then, add the onion, garlic, ginger and heat it until the onion is soft.
2. Add all the ground spice, heat them together until they have released their aroma, at about one minute. Then, deglaze the pot with the coconut milk, scraping everything from the bottom of the pot to add into the sauce. After that, add in the green chilies, tomatoes fish and Stir to coat properly.
3. Close the lid of the Instant Pot, and cook for 3 minutes on a high pressure using the 'Manual' mode. When the time is up, do a quick pressure release.
4. Add the salt and lemon juice to taste before serving. Enjoy!

70: Seafood Stew

Serves: 4 to 6 people **Prep Time:** 10 mins **Cooking Time:** 10 mins **Smart Points:** 9

Ingredients:

1. 3 tablespoons of extra-virgin olive oil
2. 2 bay leaves
3. 2 teaspoons of paprika
4. a small onion, thinly sliced
5. 1 small green bell pepper, thinly sliced
6. 1 1/2 cups of tomatoes, diced
7. 2 cloves of garlic, smashed
8. sea salt, to taste
9. pepper, grounded, to taste
10. 1 cup of fish stock
11. 1 1/2 pounds' of meaty fish, 2 inch chunks
12. 1-pound of shrimp, cleaned and deveined
13. 12 little neck clams
14. 1/4 cup of cilantro, for garnishing
15. 1 tablespoon of olive oil, for serving

Directions:

1. Using the 'Sauté' mode on the Instant Pot, add the olive oil, bay leaves, and the paprika. Stir it for 30 seconds and then add the onion, bell pepper, tomatoes, garlic, 2 tablespoons of cilantro, salt and pepper. Thereafter, stir it for a few minutes.
2. Add fish stock and water. Season the fish with salt and pepper. Nestle the clams and shrimps among the veggies in the Instant Pot. Add fish pieces to the top.
3. Close the lid tightly, and using the 'Manual' mode of the Instant Pot, cook for 10 minutes on high pressure. Once done, let the pressure naturally release.
4. Divide the stew among bowls. Drizzle with extra olive oil and sprinkle the excess cilantro and serve immediately. Enjoy!

Side Dishes

71: 1 minute Peruvian Quinoa

Serves: 4 to 6 people

Prep Time: 1 minute

Cooking Time: 1 minute

Smart Points: 7

Ingredients:

1. 1 cup of quinoa, rinsed well
2. 1 pinch of salt, or more if desired
3. 1 1/2 cups of water
4. 1 lime, squeezed and zested

Directions:

1. In the Instant Pot, add the quinoa, salt, lime, and water. Cover the lid, let it cook for 1 minute on a high pressure 'Manual' mode and when it is done, let the pressure naturally release.
2. Mix with lime juice and season it with any additional salt. Serve with seasonal veggies. Enjoy!

72: Instant Cheese Sauce

Serves: 4 to 5 people

Prep Time: 5 minutes

Cooking Time: 5 minutes

Smart Points: 6

Ingredients:

1. 2 cup of potatoes, peeled and chopped
2. 1 cup of carrot, chopped
3. 1/2 cup of yellow onion, chopped
4. 3 cloves of garlic, peeled and left whole
5. 1/2 cup of nutritional yeast
6. 1/2 cup of raw cashews
7. 1 teaspoon of turmeric
8. 1 teaspoon of salt
9. 2 cups of water

Directions:

1. Place all the ingredients in the Instant Pot, then cook for 5 minutes on a high pressure using the 'Manual' mode. Once done, do a quick pressure release and transfer all the mixture to a blender, then blend until it gets creamy.
2. Serve it with pasta, vegetables or as a dip. Enjoy!

73: Bulgar Pilaf

Serves: 4 to 6 people

Prep Time: 6 minutes

Cooking Time: 12 minutes

Smart Points: 7

Ingredients:

1. 1 tablespoon of olive oil
2. 1 tablespoon of butter
3. 3 tablespoons of onion, finely chopped
4. 1 cup of a medium sized bulgur wheat
5. 2 cups of chicken broth
6. 1/2 teaspoon of table salt
7. 1/2 teaspoon of Italian seasoning
8. lime wedges, for garnishing
9. chopped cashews, for garnishing

Directions:

1. Add the olive oil, butter into the Instant Pot and using the 'Sauté' mode, cook it until the butter melts. Add the onion, celery while cooking and stirring constantly for 2 minutes. Add the bulger, chicken broth and Italian seasoning.
2. Secure the lid and change the mode to 'Rice'. Cook on a low pressure for 12 minutes and once it is done, do a quick pressure release.
3. Remove the lid, fluff pilaf with a fork and garnish it with lime wedges and chopped cashews. Enjoy!

74: Cherry and Farro Salad

Serves: 6 to 8 people

Prep Time: 10 minutes

Cooking Time: 40 minutes

Smart Points: 3

Ingredients:

1. 1 cup of whole grain Farro
2. 1 tablespoon of apple cider vinegar
3. 1 teaspoon of lemon juice
4. 1 tablespoon of olive oil
5. 1/4 teaspoon of sea salt
6. 1/2 cup of dried cherries
7. 1/4 cup of chives, or green onions, finely minced
8. 8 to 10 leaves mint, minced
9. 2 cups of cherries, cut in half

Directions:

1. Add 3 cups of Farro into the Instant Pot and cook on a high pressure for 40 minutes using the 'Manual' mode. Once done, do a quick pressure release.
2. Drain the Farro, and put it into a bowl. Mix it with the vinegar, lemon juice, oil, salt, dried cherries, chives and mint. Thereafter, refrigerate it until it gets cold.
3. Before serving, pour in the fresh berries. Enjoy!

75: Classic Mashed Potatoes

Serves: 4 to 8 people

Prep Time: 2 minutes

Cooking Time: 20 minutes

Smart Points: 6

Ingredients:

1. 5 to 8 potatoes
2. 2 cups of water
3. 1 teaspoon of salt
4. 1/3 cup of cream
5. salt and pepper, to taste

Directions:

1. Add the potatoes, water and salt into the Instant Pot. Cover the lid and cook it for 20 minutes on a high pressure using the 'Manual' mode.
2. Once done, transfer the potatoes into a mixing bowl, remove the skins and clean it thoroughly. Add 2 tablespoons of the cooking liquid, two of the cream and start mashing with a potato masher.
3. Keep mashing while adding small quantities of the liquid and cream just until you reach the desired state. Thereafter, add the salt and pepper to taste. Serve and enjoy!

76: Creamy Mashed Sweet Potatoes

Serves: 2 to 4 people

Prep Time: 5 minutes

Cooking Time: 20 minutes

Smart Points: 4

Ingredients:

1. 2 pounds of sweet potatoes, cut into 1 inch chunks
2. 2 to 3 tablespoons of butter
3. 2 tablespoons of maple syrup
4. 1/4 teaspoon of nutmeg
5. 1 cup of cold water
6. sea salt, to taste

Directions:

1. Pour the cold water and potato chunks into the Instant Pot. Cover the lid and cook on a high pressure for 8 minutes using the 'Manual' mode. Once done, do a quick pressure release.
2. Place the cooked sweet potatoes into a large bowl and mash them partially. Add the nutmeg, butter, maple syrup and keep mashing until you reach your desired look.
3. Season it with the salt to enhance the flavors. Serve and Enjoy!

77: Garlic and Chive Mashed Potatoes

Serves: 5 people

Prep Time: 8minutes

Cooking Time: 9 minutes

Smart Points: 5

Ingredients:

1. 2 cups of chicken stock
2. 2 pounds of peeled Yukon potatoes
3. 4 cloves garlic, peeled
4. 1 cup of plain Greek yogurt
5. 1/2 cup of whole milk
6. 1/2 teaspoon of salt
7. 1/4 cup of chives, freshly chopped

Directions:

1. Mix the broth, potatoes, garlic into the Instant Pot and cook on a high pressure for 9 minutes using the 'Manual' setting. Once done, do a quick pressure release.
2. Mash the potato with a potato masher until you reach the desired state. Pour in the milk, salt and yogurt. Thereafter, add the chives just before serving. Enjoy!

78: Instant Roasted Potatoes

Serves: 4 to 6 people

Prep Time: 1 minute

Cooking Time: 24 minutes

Smart Points: 7

Ingredients:

1. 4 to 8 potatoes
2. 2 tablespoons of olive oil
3. kosher salt, to taste
4. black pepper, to taste

Directions:

1. Clean the potatoes, and makes small holes using a fork. Add one cup of cold water and the potatoes into the Instant Pot. Cover the lid and cook on a high pressure for 12 minutes using the 'Manual' mode.
2. Serve the piping hot with butter, kosher salt and the grounded black pepper. Serve and Enjoy!

79: Lemony English Peas

Serves: 4 to 6 people

Prep Time: 1 minute

Cooking Time: 3 minutes

Smart Points: 5

Ingredients:

1. 1 to 2 cloves of garlic, minced
2. 2 cups of English peas, fresh or frozen
3. 2 cups of asparagus, cut into 2 inch pieces
4. 1/2 cup of vegetable broth
5. 1 lemon, juiced and zested
6. 2 to 3 tablespoons of pine nuts, toasted

Directions:

1. Add the garlic, peas, asparagus and the vegetable broth into the Instant Pot. Cook on a low pressure for 2 minutes using the 'Manual' mode.
2. Add the lemon zest, juice and stir. Then transfer it to a large bowl and garnish it with the pine nuts. Enjoy!

80: Maple Glazed Carrots

Serves: 4 people

Prep Time: 5 minutes

Cooking Time: 4 minutes

Smart Points: 5

Ingredients:

1. 2 pounds' of carrots, peeled and thickly sliced
2. 1/4 cup of raisins
3. 1 cup of water
4. 1 tablespoon of maple syrup
5. 1 tablespoon of butter
6. pepper, to taste

Directions:

1. Put the carrots, raisins and the water into the Instant Pot, then cook for 4 minutes on a high pressure using the 'Manual' mode. Once the time is up, do a quick release of the pressure through the valve.
2. Strain the carrots, while the carrots are straining, melt the butter and maple the syrup into the Instant Pot.
3. Mix properly, tumble in the carrots,raisins and coat it with butter and sauce. Serve with freshly grounded pepper. Enjoy!

81: Mexican Polenta

Serves: 3 to 6 people

Prep Time: 5 minutes

Cooking Time: 15 minutes

Smart Points: 7

Ingredients:

1. 1 cup of green onion, sliced
2. 2 teaspoons of garlic, minced
3. 2 cups of vegetable broth
4. 2 cups of boiling water
5. 1 cup of corn meal, grits
6. 1/4 cups of cilantro, fresh and chopped
7. 1 tablespoon of chili powder
8. 1 teaspoon of cumin
9. 1 teaspoon of oregano
10. 1/2 teaspoon of smoked paprika
11. 1/4 teaspoon of cayenne pepper

Directions:

1. Using the 'Sauté' mode in the Instant Pot, heat the green onion and the minced garlic until it produces some fragrance, while only adding a small amount of water. Then,pour in the vegetable broth, water, corn meal, cilantro, spices and stir to mix properly.
2. Cover the lid and cook on a high pressure for 5 minutes using the 'Manual' mode. Once done, do a quick pressure release. Serve as it is, or place it in a glass dish alongside with other recipes. Enjoy!

82: One Pot Brussels Sprouts

Serves: 4 to 6 people

Prep Time: 10 minutes

Cooking Time: 20 minutes

Smart Points: 6

Ingredients:

1. 5 slices of bacon, chopped
2. 6 cups of Brussel sprouts, chopped
3. 1/4 teaspoon of salt
4. 2 tablespoons of water
5. 2 tablespoons of balsamic reduction
6. 1/4 cup of goat cheese, optional
7. pepper, to taste

Directions:

1. Using the 'Sauté' mode of the Instant Pot, add the chopped bacon. Heat it until the desired crispiness is reached. Thereafter, add the chopped Brussel sprouts and stir to cover with the flavorful bacon fat.
2. Add the water and sprinkle it with salt and pepper. Then cover it, stir, every few minutes and replace the lid. Then continue to heat it uncovered until the Brussels crisps up.
3. Transfer it to a serving dish, top it with the balsamic reduction and goat cheese. Enjoy!

83: Perfect Mashed Potatoes and Parsnips

Serves: 6 people

Prep Time: 5 minutes

Cooking Time: 12 minutes

Smart Points: 7

Ingredients:

1. 3 pounds of Yukon gold potatoes, peeled and cut into 1 1/2 inch cubes
2. 1 pound of parsnips, cut into 1-inch-thick circles
3. 1 teaspoon of pepper
4. 1 teaspoon of salt
5. 4 tablespoons of butter, room temperature
6. 4 tablespoons of half-and-half

Directions:

1. Pour 2 cups of water into the inner pot of the Instant Pot. Place the steamer basket in the pot, add the potatoes and parsnips into it.
2. Cover the Instant Pot's lid and cook on a high pressure for 7 minutes using the 'Manual' mode. Once the time is up, do a quick pressure release.
3. Open the Instant Pot and remove the steamer basket. Sprinkle it with salt and pepper. Using a potato masher, mash the potatoes and the parsnips, thereafter add the butter and half-and-half. Then mix properly.
4. Garnish it with the fresh herbs if desired. Enjoy!

84: Cranberry Sauce

Serves: 3 people

Prep Time: 5 minutes

Cooking Time: 15 minutes

Smart Points: 5

Ingredients:

1. 12 ounces' of cranberries, rinsed and stems removed
2. 2 1/2 teaspoons of orange zest
3. 1/4 cup of orange juice, freshly squeezed
4. 2 tablespoons of maple syrup, or honey
5. pinch of salt
6. 1/2 to 1 cup of white sugar

Directions:

1. Mix the maple syrup, orange juice and pour it into the Instant Pot. Add the lemon zest, 10 ounces' of cranberries and reserve the other 2 ounces for later use.
2. Close the lid and cook on a high pressure for 1 minutes using the 'Manual' mode. Once done, let the pressure naturally release for 7 minutes.
3. Switch the mode to 'sauté' and break the cranberries with a spoon. Then, add the white sugar, the remaining cranberries and stir. By that time,the heat will instantly melt the sugar to form a thick cranberry sauce, which will require you to add a pinch of salt.
4. Serve hot or cold with your favorite dish. Enjoy!

85: Hard-Boiled Eggs

Serves: 3 to 6 people

Prep Time: 1 minutes

Cooking Time: 5 minutes

Smart Points: 5

Ingredients:

1. 1 to 6 eggs
2. 1 cup of water, cold only
3. Salt and pepper, to taste

Directions:

1. Fill the Instant Pot with one cup of cold water. Place the eggs, lock the lid and cook for 5 minutes on a high pressure using the 'Manual' mode. When the time is up, do a quick pressure release.
2. Place the the eggs into a container filled with cold water. Keep the water cool by consistently adding more water from the sink. If you want to serve it warm, cool it for 1 minute and if cold, then cool it off for 3 minutes.
3. Tap the 2 ends and the middle of the egg to peel delicately, then sprinkle the pepper and salt on top it. Serve it with other morning food and enjoy!

86: Red, White and Green Brussel Sprouts

Serves: 4 people

Prep Time: 10 minutes

Cooking Time: 3 minutes

Smart Points: 4

Ingredients:

1. 1 pound of Brussel Sprouts
2. 1/4 cup of pine nuts, toasted
3. 1 pomegranate
4. 1 tablespoon of extra-virgin olive oil
5. 1/2 teaspoon
6. 1 grate pepper

Directions:

1. Remove the leaves, stems, of the Brussel Sprouts and cut the large ones in half so that all of them will be of equal size. Prepare the Instant Pot by pouring one cup of water and adding a steamer basket. Thereafter, put the sprouts in the basket.
2. Cover the lid and cook for 3 minutes on a high pressure using the 'Manual' mode. When the time is up, let the pressure naturally release.
3. Move the sprouts into a dish and dress in the olive oil, salt and pepper prior to sprinkling toasted pine nuts and the pomegranate seeds. Serve at a room temperature. Enjoy!

87: Roasted Baby Potatoes

Serves: 4 to 6 people

Prep Time: 1 minute

Cooking Time: 20 minutes

Smart Points: 7

Ingredients:

1. 5 tablespoons of vegetable oil
2. 2 pounds of fingerling potatoes, or small baby potatoes
3. 1 sprig rosemary
4. 3 cloves of garlic
5. 1 cup of stock
6. salt, to taste
7. pepper, to taste

Directions:

1. Preheat the Instant Pot using the 'sauté' mode, and add the potatoes, garlic and rosemary. Roll the potatoes around to cook them on both sides.
2. Using a knife, pierce the potatoes in the middle. Pour in the stock and cover the lid. Cook it on a high pressure for 11 minutes using the 'Manual' mode. Once done, quickly release the pressure.
3. Remove the outer skin of the cloves and serve it wholely or mashed with the potatoes. Then, sprinkle the salt and pepper on top of it. Enjoy!

88: Smokey Sweet Potato Mash

Serves: 4 people

Prep Time: 10 minutes

Cooking Time: 11 minutes

Smart Points: 4

Ingredients:

1. 1 cup of water
2. 3 medium sized sweet potatoes, scrubbed
3. 1/4 cup of butter
4. 1/4 cup l of light brown sugar, packed
5. 1/2 teaspoon of smoked paprika
6. 1/4 teaspoon of table salt
7. 4 bacon sliced, cooked and crumbled

Directions:

1. Place the steam rack into the Instant Pot and pour in some water. Place the potatoes in the rack. And cover the lid while cooking on a high pressure for 11 to 14 minutes using the 'Manual' mode. Once done, do a quick pressure release.
2. When it gets cool enough, peel the potatoes and place it in a large bowl. Mash it roughly and pour in the butter, sugar, salt and paprika. Thereafter, sprinkle it with the crumbled bacon and serve immediately. Enjoy!

89: Thick Nacho Cheese Sauce

Serves: 4 people

Prep Time: 10 minutes

Cooking Time: 15 minutes

Smart Points: 7

Ingredients:

1. 2 cups of potatoes, cubed
2. 1 cup of yellow onion, chopped
3. 1 cup of carrot, chopped
4. 1/2 jar roasted red bell peppers
5. 1/2 cup of cashews
6. 2 cups of water
7. 1/3 cup of nutritional yeast
8. 1 tablespoon of Dijon mustard
9. 2 teaspoons of lemon juice
10. 1 teaspoon of salt
11. 1/4 teaspoon of liquid smoke

Directions:

1. Add the potatoes, onions, carrots, cashews, and water into the Instant Pot. Cover the lid and while using the 'Manual' mode, cook for 2 minutes at a high pressure. Once done, let the pressure naturally release.
2. Using a spoon, transfer the vegetable mixture and liquid to a blender. Add the nutritional yeast, mustard, lemon juice, salt, liquid smoke and blend until it gets smooth and creamy. Serve and enjoy!

90: Corn on the Cob

Serves: 4 people

Prep Time: 5 minutes

Cooking Time: 20 minutes

Smart Points: 5

Ingredients:

1. 4 ears corn, on the cob
2. 3 tablespoons of light soy sauce
3. 2 tablespoons of shacha sauce
4. 1 tablespoon of sugar
5. 1 teaspoon of garlic powder
6. 1/4 teaspoon of sesame oil

Directions:

1. Pour 1 cup of cold tap water into the Instant Pot, place a trivet into the pressure cooker and keep the corn in the trivet. Cover the lid and cook at a 'Manual' mode on a high pressure for 2 minutes. Once done, do a quick pressure release.
2. While the corn is cooking in the Instant Pot, preheat the oven to 450 degrees Fahrenheit. Mix the light soy sauce, shacha sauce, sugar, garlic powder, and 1/4 teaspoon of sesame oil in a small mixing bowl.
3. Then brush the sauce on the corn on all sides using a brush and place them on a baking tray in the oven for 5 to 10 minutes. Serve immediately and enjoy!

91: Carrot Puree

Serves: 2 to 4 people

Prep Time: 5 minutes

Cooking Time: 4 minutes

Smart Points: 3

Ingredients:

1. 1 1/2 pounds' of carrots, roughly chopped
2. 1 tablespoon of butter, room temperature
3. 1 tablespoon of honey
4. 1/4 teaspoon of sea salt
5. 1 cup of water

Directions:

1. Pour the water into the Instant Pot, and add the carrots into it. Cook for 4 minutes on a high pressure using the 'Manual' mode with the lid covered. Once done, quick release the pressure.
2. Place the carrots in a deep bowl, use a hand blender to blend the carrots until they reach the desired state. Then add butter, honey and sea salt to the puree, then mix properly.
3. Taste the carrot puree, and add the brown sugar for more sweetness if necessary. Serve immediately with the main dish. Enjoy!

92: Paleo Beet Borscht

Serves: 4 people

Prep Time: 20 minutes

Cooking Time: 45 minutes

Smart Points: 5

Ingredients:

1. 8 cups of beets
2. ½ cup of celery, diced
3. ½ cup of carrots, diced
4. 2 cloves of garlic, diced
5. 1 medium sized onion, diced
6. 3 cups of cabbage, shredded
7. 6 cups of stock, beef or chicken
8. 1 bay leaf
9. 1 tablespoon of salt
10. ½ tablespoons of thyme
11. ½ cup of dill, freshly chopped
12. ½ cup of coconut yogurt, plain

Directions:

1. Place the beets in the Instant Pot with 1 cup of water. Steam it for 7 minutes, then quick release the pressure. Drop it straight into ice cold water, as the skins will peel off by themselves.
2. Put the beets, carrots, garlic, celery, onions, bay leaf, cabbage, salt, stock and the thyme into the Instant Pot, then cook for 45 minutes using the 'Soup' mode.
3. When the time is up, allow a natural release so that the soup won't splatter.
4. Scoop the Beet Borscht into bowls, and add some dairy free yogurt. Garnish it with the fresh dill. Enjoy!

93: Instant Mexi-Cali Rice

Serves: 4 to 6 people

Prep Time: 5 minutes

Cooking Time: 5 minutes

Smart Points: 5

Ingredients:

1. 6 cups of brown rice, cooked
2. 1 can of Fire Roasted Tomatoes
3. 2 cups of salsa, homemade or branded
4. 4 tablespoons of tomato paste
5. 3 cups of onion, chopped
6. 6 cloves of garlic, finely minced
7. 1 1/2 cup of water

Directions:

1. Place all the ingredients in the Instant Pot, and cook on a high pressure for 5 minutes. When the time is up, do a quick pressure release.
2. You can pour in some chopped cilantro if you like or garnish it with any type of topping you like. Enjoy!

94: Butternut Squash Risotto

Serves: 6 to 8 people

Prep Time: 21 minutes

Cooking Time: 12 minutes

Smart Points: 4

Ingredients:

1. 2 teaspoons of olive oil
2. 1/2 cup of yellow onion, chopped
3. 1 1/2 cups of Arborio rice
4. 1 cup of water
5. 1/2 teaspoon of table salt
6. 1/4 teaspoon of black pepper, grounded
7. 3 cups of butternut squash, 3/4 inch pieces
8. 2 cans of beef broth
9. 1/2 cup of Parmigiano-Reggiano cheese
10. 3 tablespoons of unsalted butter
11. 2 tablespoons of fresh parsley, finely chopped

Directions:

1. Preheat the Instant Pot using the 'Sauté' mode, and add the oil. Thereafter add the onion and cook for 5 minutes. Then, add the rice, and cook for 1 more minute until the rice is covered with the oil.
2. Add 1/2 cup of water, salt and pepper, cook it until the water is absorbed and cover the lid, using the 'Rice' mode, on a low pressure for 12 minutes.
3. When the time is up, do a quick pressure release. Add the cheese, butter and the parsley, while still stirring until it gets creamy. Serve immediately.

95: Chicken and Pancetta Risotto

Serves: 4 people

Prep Time: 10 minutes   **Cooking Time:** 12 minutes

Smart Points: 5

Ingredients:

1. 2 cloves of garlic, chopped
2. 100 grams' of butter
3. 1 tablespoon of olive oil
4. salt and pepper, to taste
5. 50 grams' of pancetta, diced
6. 300 grams' of chicken, diced
7. 300 grams of Arborio rice
8. 4 tablespoons of parmesan, grated
9. 1/3 cup of white wine
10. 3 1/4 cups of chicken stock
11. 1 tablespoon of fresh thyme
12. lemon zest, for garnishing
13. basil leaves, for garnishing

Directions:

1. Using the 'Sauté' mode of the Instant Pot, add the oil and 30 grams of butter. Heat the onion, garlic, pancetta and chicken for 2 minutes.
2. Pour in rice, add the time and stir in the wine. Empty in the stock and stir really properly. Using the 'Manual' mode, cook on a high pressure for 12 minutes.
3. At the end of the time, quick release the pressure. Stir the risotto well to form a creamy texture and pour in the grated Parmesan. Then, leave it to stand for 3 minutes.
4. Serve the topped with an extra Parmesan, freshly grounded pepper, grated lemon zest and the basil leaves. Enjoy!

96: Confetti Basmati Rice

Serves: 4 to 6 people

Prep Time: 5 minutes

Cooking Time: 5 minutes

Smart Points: 5

Ingredients:

1. 1 tablespoon of olive oil
2. 1 medium sized onion, chopped
3. 1 bell pepper, any color
4. 1 carrot, grated
5. water, as needed in the recipe directions
6. 2 cups of basmati rice, or long-grain rice
7. 1/2 cup of peas, frozen
8. 1 teaspoon of salt

Directions:

1. Preheat the Instant Pot using the 'Sauté' mode. Add the oil, onion and heat it until it becomes translucent. In the meantime, using a 4 cup capacity liquid container, add the bell pepper, grated carrots and pat lightly into an even layer.
2. Pour the water into the container until all the ingredients reach the 3 cup mark and set it aside. Back to the Instant Pot, pour in the rice, peas, salt and mix properly.
3. Add the measuring cup with the water and veggies into the Instant Pot and cover the lid. Cook it for 3 minutes on a high pressure using the 'Manual' mode.
4. When the time is up, let the pressure naturally release, fluff the rice with a fork, serve and enjoy!

97: Fluffy Jasmine Rice

Serves: 4 people

Prep Time: 1 minute

Cooking Time: 15 minutes

Smart Points: 5

Ingredients:

1. 2 1/2 cup of water
2. 2 cup of Jasmine rice
3. 1/2 teaspoon of sea salt, optional

Directions:

1. Add the water, rice , salt, the Instant Pot and cover ie with a glass lid. Then, using the 'Sauté' mode, boil the water.
2. Now press the 'Keep Warm/Cancel' twice to cancel the sauté mode and activate the keep warm mode. Use the keep warm timer for 9 minutes, and after that,, cancel the keep warm mode.
3. Fluff the rice with a fork before serving. Enjoy!

98: Perfect Brown Rice

Serves: 4 people

Prep Time: 1 minute

Cooking Time: 22 minutes

Smart Points: 3

Ingredients:

1. 2 cups of brown rice
2. 2 1/2 cups of water

Directions:

1. Add the rice, water to the Instant Pot and secure the lid. Cook on a 'Manual' mode for 22 minutes on a high pressure. When the time is up, let the pressure naturally release.
2. Serve alongside your favorite main dishes. Enjoy!

99: Pasta Caprese

Serves: 3 people

Prep Time: 5 minutes   **Cooking Time:** 10 minutes

Smart Points: 4

Ingredients:

1. 2 1/2 cups of mezze penne
2. 1 onion, thinly sliced
3. 1 tablespoon of olive oil
4. 1 can of tomato sauce
5. 6 garlic cloves, minced
6. 1 cup of grape tomatoes, halved
7. 4 handfuls basil leaves
8. ¼ cup of balsamic vinegar
9. 1 teaspoon salt
10. 1 teaspoon of red pepper, optional
11. Parmesan Cheese, optional
12. 1 cup of mozzarella balls, fresh
13. 1 cup of water

Directions:

1. Adjust the Instant Pot to 'the Sauté' mode and add the onion, oil, garlic and red pepper. Heat it for one minute, then add the grape tomatoes, pasta, pasta sauce, half of the basil leaves, water and stir evenly.
2. Seal the lid of the Instant Pot and cook on a high pressure for 4 minutes using the 'Manual' setting. Once done, do a quick pressure release, add the mozzarella cheese and vinegar.
3. Serve it hot and garnish it with the chopped basil and shredded Parmesan. Enjoy!

100: Macaroni and Cheese

Serves: 8 people

Prep Time: 5 minutes

Cooking Time: 6 minutes

Smart Points: 7

Ingredients:

1. 1-pound of elbow macaroni
2. 4 cups of chicken broth
3. 12 ounces' of Cheddar Cheese, shredded
4. 3 tablespoons of unsalted butter
5. ½ cup of Parmesan Cheese, shredded
6. ½ cup of sour cream
7. 1/8 teaspoon of cayenne pepper
8. 1 ½ teaspoons of yellow mustard

Directions:

1. Mix the macaroni, broth and butter into the Instant Pot. Cover the lid and cook it on a high pressure for 6 minutes using the 'Manual' mode. Once done, do a quick pressure release.
2. Open the pot and pour in the cheeses, sour cream, cayenne pepper and mustard. Let the mixture thicken for 5 minutes, then serve. Enjoy!

101: Minestrone Soup

Serves: 4 to 6 people

Prep Time: 5 minutes

Cooking Time: 20 minutes

Smart Points: 6

Ingredients:

1. 1 cup of beans, cooked
2. 1-pound of ground beef, browned
3. 1 potato, diced
4. 2 carrots, diced
5. 2 stalks celery, diced
6. 1 onion
7. 2 cloves of garlic
8. 32 ounces' of chicken broth
9. 28 ounces' of tomatoes, crushed
10. 2 teaspoon of tomato paste
11. 2 tablespoon of Italian Seasoning
12. 1 teaspoon of salt

Directions:

1. Mix all the ingredients in the Instant Pot and close the lid. Cook at a 'Manual' mode for 20 minutes on a high pressure. Once done, let the pressure naturally release for 10 minutes, then do a quick release.
2. Serve and enjoy!

The Final Words

Hope you like this small, but helpful cookbook for a topic not discussed in the food category too often. An instant pot is definitely a great addition to the everyday kitchen arsenal of both men and women, and taking the health benefits into note, you can say that it is the best choice for a cooking appliance! So, if you have an instant pot and an empty stomach, go ahead and try a recipe out today! Hope you will have your ideal weight by following weight watchers program!

Thanks for buying this book, your support is what keeps me going!

Made in the USA
Middletown, DE
18 January 2018